LOCAL HISTORY TODAY

Papers Presented at Three 1979 Regional
Workshops for Local Historical
Organizations in Indiana

David J. Russo
Dorothy Weyer Creigh
Roger Fortin
John J. Newman
Pamela J. Bennett

with an introduction by Thomas K. Krasean

Indianapolis
Indiana Historical Society

David J. Russo is Associate Professor of History in McMaster University, Hamilton, Ontario, Canada

Dorothy Weyer Creigh is Director of the Publications Division of the Adams County (Nebraska) Historical Society

Roger Fortin is Associate Academic Vice-President in Xavier University, Cincinnati, Ohio

John J. Newman is Head of the Archives Division of the Indiana Commission on Public Records

Pamela J. Bennett is Director of the Indiana Historical Bureau

Copies of *Local History Today* are for sale by the Indiana Historical Society, 315 West Ohio Street, Indianapolis, Indiana 46202 for $1.50 per copy.

CONTENTS

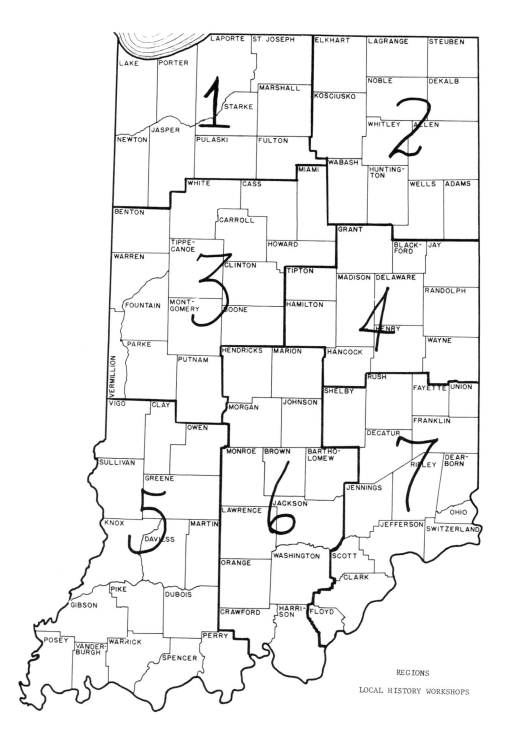

REGIONS

LOCAL HISTORY WORKSHOPS

Introduction

The papers in this publication constitute the second volume of *Local History Today*,* a series of lectures presented at three regional workshops for local historical societies and organizations in Indiana. The two-day workshops were held in 1979 and were co-sponsored by the Indiana Historical Bureau.

The workshop theme was conceived and developed by the co-sponsors who were concerned about the plight of history at the grassroots level, which, among other things, found many local historical societies continuing in the traditional "meeting and eating" program format that was devoid of the common purpose of such gatherings, i.e., the study and promotion of their local or community history. With the rumblings of the country's bicentennial celebration still to be heard in the background, we decided in early 1977 that it was an appropriate time to offer the local societies an opportunity to upgrade their present programs by providing them with a variety of workshop sessions covering new trends and techniques in the realm of historical society work. The workshops were a combination of lectures, slide presentations, and hands-on demonstrations, covering seven or eight different

* The first volume of *Local History Today*, Papers Presented at Four Regional Workshops for Local Historical Organizations in Indiana, June, 1978-April, 1979, was published by the Indiana Historical Society in 1979.

topics that included: funding for the local society, conservation of museum artifacts and library materials, oral history, historic preservation, publications, operating a small museum, and several others. (A more detailed description of the workshop format can be found in the introduction to the first volume of *Local History Today*.)

Highlighting each workshop program was a keynote address presented by a noted historian or scholar in the field of local history. Once again, we believed that the importance of local history needed to be emphasized and how better to accomplish this welcome task than to invite a trained historian to present a paper underlining the significance of local history in relation to the history of our state and nation? This then is the central theme of *Local History Today*.

Papers presented and published in the first volume were "Midwestern Transformation: From Traditional Pioneers to Modern Society," by Richard Jensen, Newberry Library; "After the Bicentennial and *Roots:* What Next? Local History at the Crossroads," by Robert M. Sutton, University of Illinois; "Local History: A Mainspring for National History," by Thomas D. Clark, Emeritus Professor, University of Kentucky; and "Above-Ground Archaeology: Discovering a Community's History through Local Artifacts," by Thomas J. Schlereth, University of Notre Dame.

This second volume contains the last three keynote lectures plus two papers that were presented at all seven workshops by two of the workshop personnel, Pamela J. Bennett, director, Indiana Historical Bureau, and John J. Newman, state archivist. Both articles deal with Indiana-related topics but have potential reference value for other states as well. Dr. David J. Russo was to have presented the keynote address at the Lafayette Workshop, held June 15-16, but due to problems in flight schedules, Dr. Russo was unable to reach Lafayette. Dr. John Stover, Purdue University, spoke in his place. (Dr. Russo later presented his paper at the Society's annual meeting in Indianapolis on November 3.) Mrs. Dorothy W. Creigh delivered her paper before the participants attending the sixth workshop held at Anderson College, September 7-8. Dr. Roger Fortin spoke before the seventh and last workshop held October 26-27, at the Sisters of St. Francis Convent, Oldenburg.

The following is a list of individuals who presented one or more programs at the final three workshops:

Pamela J. Bennett, director, Indiana Historical Bureau
Robert Kirby, director, Indiana Junior Historical Society
J. Reid Williamson, executive director, Historic Landmarks Foundation of Indiana
John Harris, director, Tippecanoe County Historical Association
Diane Alpert, museum consultant
Esther Dittlinger, Anderson Public Library
Howard Eldon, curator, Indiana Room, Anderson Public Library
Debra Fausset, assistant director, Indiana Junior Historical Society
Bobbie Garver, grants co-ordinator, Indiana Arts Commission
Gerald Handfield, field representative, Indiana State Library
Denver Howlett, chief, exhibits production, Indiana State Museum
Andrea Pactor, museum co-ordinator, Indiana Arts Commission
Craig Leonard, architectural historian
Nancy Long, architectural historian, Indiana State Museum
Pamela Najar, conservator, Indiana Historical Society
John J. Newman, state archivist, State Commission on Public Records
Mark Rozeen, co-ordinator, Resource Center, Indiana Committee for the Humanities
Pat Steele, curator, Huddleston Farmhouse Inn Museum
Carol Waddell, assistant director, Tippecanoe County Historical Association

A special thanks to the following individuals for their part in promoting the workshop program and helping to insure its success: Gayle Thornbrough, Executive Secretary, Indiana Historical Society, for her continued and valuable advice and support; Pamela J. Bennett who served as co-director of the workshop; Dan Kiernan of the Society staff; Lisa Ballard, Indiana Historical Bureau; and Lisa Nowak and Paula Corpuz of the Society's editorial staff.

Finally to all of the participants who attended the workshops, and the many who assisted in local arrangements, we dedicate this work to you.

Thomas K. Krasean
Workshop Director

Some Impressions of the Nonacademic Local Historians and Their Writings

David J. Russo

I suppose it seems natural that an American historian who was born and raised in Deerfield, Massachusetts, would at some point in his career turn his attention to the study of local history. For anyone who grew up in Deerfield in the 1950s, "history" was palpable, inescapable. A casual stroll down the elm-lined main street took one past the growing number of eighteenth-century houses carefully restored, furnished, and opened for public inspection by Henry and Helen Flynt. Tours by "townspeople" were always free of charge, which was also the case in the local historical society's Memorial Hall museum, with its antique furnishings and agricultural implements—a whole world of ancient artifacts. Even the old burying ground at the rear of Deerfield Academy's colonial-styled buildings had an air of "olden times" about it.

I grew up in this setting, with "history" in my bones. But the history I learned at the nearby state university was of another kind. American history was national history, mainly a chronology of political events and crises. Both as an undergraduate research assistant and, later, as a doctoral student at Yale I studied and wrote about national politics. Deerfield seemed far away and quite irrelevant to my concerns as a "serious" student of the American past. But, as a young instructor charged with the responsibility of lecturing in U.S. survey courses, I became convinced that something was fundamentally wrong with the textbooks I felt compelled to assign my students. History, I insisted, should involve the study of *all* significant aspects of the life of a people, not just politics, not just what governments did. How could I seriously be expected to believe that all of American life

1

changed with, say, a change in the presidency, thus producing a "Jeffersonian Period," a "Jacksonian Period"? Why
should the American past be chopped up by administrations?
What of importance changed when Monroe followed Madi-
son, Fillmore followed Taylor, Hayes followed Grant, Coo-
lidge followed Harding? Why should I assume that archi-
tecture, art, thought, science, medicine, even social class
structure or economic development evolved in lock-step fashion with politics? Indeed, why not view the political system
as something that *reflected* the more basic arrangements of
American life?

I was in this frame of mind when, in 1970, the Flynts
built a new library to house the local historical society's extensive manuscript collection relating to Deerfield's past.
My examination of the well-equipped new facility was a significant turning point in my scholarly life because it immediately became apparent that the materials were extensive
enough to provide what I felt was a magnificent opportunity
for the preparation of a full-scale history of the town. When
my university granted me a sabbatical leave of absence, I
gladly committed myself to such a project.

As I read the scholarship on the history of American towns
before starting research on Deerfield itself, it suddenly occurred to me that the American past could be more clearly
and comprehensively understood if it were examined from
the vantage points of the various levels of groups and communities that all Americans have lived in simultaneously—
families; rural areas, towns, or cities; states; regions; as well
as the nation. I found that much recent scholarship supported the theme that American life was largely organized
at the level of the family and local community in colonial
times and that the mass society of our time emerged in piece-
meal fashion during the eighteenth, nineteenth, and early
twentieth centuries. So, through most of American history,
the primary group or community, the one that most significantly shaped American lives, was the family, the town, the
city, to some extent the state and region, but only recently the
nation. With the excitement of anyone who believes he has
made a great discovery, I sketched out the new scheme that

I believed should guide American historical study and found that the American Association for State and Local History was interested in publishing what emerged as a freewheeling, speculative, new synthesis. The result was *Families and Communities*.

I wish that I could report to you that *Families and Communities* quickly became recognized as the landmark statement I—perhaps naively—thought it was. The general response of reviewers and correspondents has been mixed, and I myself now feel that perhaps the thesis is either too complicated and cumbersome to serve as a blueprint for scholarship or does not go far enough in spelling out just how those writing on the American past can relate their work to the master scheme. Indeed, I have continued to think about the matters discussed in the book and would, if ever given the opportunity of preparing a second edition, significantly revise the original version. Such is the nature of synthesizing on a grand scale.

I remain convinced that the basic themes of *Families and Communities* are sound, even though I have begun to wonder if historical study somehow has to have the simplicity—and the distortions—that come from a single focus—the nation and its government. Perhaps the concept of *levels* of groups and communities is too confusing or complicated ever to be widely accepted as a guide for the study of a people. And yet, I still believe that my approach, if followed, would lead to a far greater understanding of the American past than the outline fixed in college textbooks without significant alteration since the 1920s.

In any case, I launched the research on Deerfield at the beginning of my sabbatical year with great optimism, convinced that the history of any town—but especially one's hometown—was of scholarly significance, if only the scheme in *Families and Communities* were kept in mind. By the end of my leave I had examined family papers of all kinds, the reports of various organizations and town agencies, as well as area newspaper files, and had even interviewed a sizable number of the townspeople for their historical recollections. But, as I returned to my teaching duties, something hap-

pened: enthusiasm faded; I turned to other, but related
projects involving local history. Gradually, the reason for
my delay (or avoidance) became apparent to me: I did not
have a distinctive theme or approach to the study of Deerfield's history. In the meantime, the scholarship on American
towns was increasing rapidly. The time had passed, I felt, for
just another book on just another town, modeled after earlier
scholarly efforts. In other words, I had somehow lost a justification for further research on Deerfield, unless I wanted
to present a history of the place out of sheer curiosity or love,
something that would be read, not by students and scholars,
but by those who lived in, knew, or cared about Deerfield.

This, after all, is what had motivated *non*academic local
historians since the early nineteenth century. Deerfield's
own "antiquarian," George Sheldon, wrote a massive, two-
volume history of the town during the 1880s and 1890s,
founded and led the local historical society for nearly five
decades, and brought together the artifacts and documents
that now fill the museum in Memorial Hall and the Flynt
Library next door. I had examined Sheldon's papers and had
long been curious to find out how typical or distinctive he
was. Since I had reached an impasse in my own work, perhaps it would be useful to study the nonacademic historians,
my predecessors, those who had written practically all the
local history Americans had read until very recently. If the
town or city was the central community in the lives of Americans through much of American history, what view did
Americans have of local history as reflected in the work of
these amateur historians? A new project took shape as I prepared for another sabbatical leave.

*   *   *

During this past school year, I have examined hundreds
of volumes of local history, and, out of this work, I have
formed some impressions of the amateur town and city historians and their histories. I'd like to emphasize that what
I'm about to say is impressionistic and that any number of
these tentative observations may well be revised in the future
as a result of further research. I believe that a progress re-

port on current projects has a place in a gathering of this kind, however.

I decided to work from the west coast to the east coast, state by state—west to east, because I felt that, since much of the best historical scholarship in the field of American local history has been focused on the eastern states, especially on New England, I should avoid the charge that what I had to say is restricted to, say, eastern Massachusetts; state by state, because I felt that, since much scholarship involves a small sampling of states or regions, I should try to avoid the charge that my conclusions are based on material that is somehow uncharacteristic or atypical. Though I've become bleary-eyed in the process, I'm glad in retrospect I chose the method just outlined: there really is no substitute for looking at the whole thing, especially when you can do so from a single vantage point, in this case, the local history collection of the Library of Congress in Washington.

My first observation is that nonacademic town and city histories are very unevenly distributed across the country. It would be misleading and an exaggeration to claim that such writing is largely a New England phenomenon, but there is only one area in the union where there has been an almost geographically continuous production of town and city histories, and that area is New England, especially Massachusetts, something that ironically, *supports* the geographic imbalance in historical scholarship I mentioned a moment ago. Cities everywhere have been the subject of amateur histories, but not towns. Indeed, the farther away from Massachusetts a small community is, the less likely it is that someone has written its history, though the populous west coast is somewhat of an exception to this rule.

Why some local communities are the subject of histories and others are not is something I cannot answer at present, but there undoubtedly are many answers. In fact, generalizations of any kind on this overall topic are hard to come by, for the antiquarians, it seems, had little sense of themselves as a group, were certainly without any formal organization beyond the state level, and though there have always been widely recognized models of good local history, the amateur

historian has never felt compelled to imitate slavishly anyone else's work. The whole enterprise has been a loosely
structured one, something entirely in keeping with the fact
that these histories have been focused on particular towns
and cities, on that which makes a place Hoboken, New
Jersey, or Eureka, California, and no other place on earth.

I should amend my earlier remark about towns without
histories to some extent: most towns have had historical
sketches written about them, sketches that have appeared in
county histories. I have not yet examined this other form of
local historical writing because I—perhaps myopically—
have until now fixed my gaze on full-scale town and city
histories. At least in its heyday—from the Civil War to World
War I—the county history, with its town-by-town sketches,
was certainly produced with greater geographic uniformity
across the country than the histories to which I've paid attention.

That the full-scale local history was nurtured in New
England, and particularly in Massachusetts, is indisputable,
I think. Why this was so has everything to do with the earlier
history of that area, so that to comment intelligently on the
question of origins, one needs to be familiar with the overall
history of colonial New England. One needs to know, in
short, about the context within which this particular genre of
writing emerged. Towns were a very special human creation
for the Puritans. The original white settlers of each township
in colonial Massachusetts pledged to form a community
dedicated to and in the service of God. Puritan ministers
later wrote histories of these settlements, placing them
within the wider framework of a divine drama involving God
and his chosen people.[1] It was a natural development for
Congregational ministers to write the earliest recognizably
secular histories in the 1820s, 1830s, and 1840s, though the
timing of such a shift cannot be easily explained. Drawing
on relatively well-kept church and town records, these pioneering antiquarians presented a series of "civil" and "eccle-
siastical" accounts of various Massachusetts towns, fanning
out from Boston.

My state-by-state survey has turned out to be quite sensible in that the origins and development of local historical writing, I've found, varied considerably from state to state, even in the case of adjoining states with similar periods of initial white settlement. Sometimes individuals presented themselves as *the* pioneer with varying degrees of fanfare and self-advertisement. Frances Caulkins maintained that her *History of Norwich (Conn.)* (1845) "is not founded on previous histories,—it has no predecessor . . . it is an independent, original work. . . ."[2] In other cases, local, county, or state historical societies were instrumental in fostering the earliest projects in a given state. For example, in Vermont, the Historical Society of Middlebury in 1846 appointed a committee to investigate the feasibility of finding people to write histories of the various towns in the county. This committee appointed competent agents in the several towns and sent to them circulars, embracing the plan recommended by the society.[3] In states such as Massachusetts, New Jersey, Pennsylvania, Maryland, Wisconsin, and Washington, it is clear that the state historical society played a key role in the early development of local historical writing, providing a repository for material, a forum for the publication of pieces shorter or narrower than full-scale town or city histories, and even officials who themselves became well-known antiquarians for certain communities (like Mayer Brantz of Baltimore, John Watson of Philadelphia, Clarence Bagley of Seattle, or Clarence Burton of Detroit).

Even though there has always been a considerable variety in the overall format and design of amateur local historical writing, certain basic forms have been at least typical of certain periods of time, though there has always been considerable overlapping. The first form to typify this genre of writing was the annals, that is, a listing or description of events presented in chronological order, year by year. Some of the earliest recognizably secular histories assumed this form.[4] Though I can't prove or demonstrate the connection, it seems to me that these annals evolved out of the efforts of colonial printers to provide a chronology of events on a daily or weekly basis in their early journals or newspapers. Just as the pioneering journalists tried to provide what they

called a "history of their times," so too did the annalists try
to provide a retrospective collection of events extending over
a long period, arranged much as they had been in the colonial
press, but with one crucial difference: the early journalists
ordinarily did not focus on *local* happenings, whereas the
annalists, of course, did—exclusively so.

But "the annals" form did not typify local historical writing for very long, and in the 1830s, 1840s, and 1850s, in
Massachusetts, the Congregational ministers developed the
quasi-civil, quasi-ecclesiastical histories already referred to,
histories still characterized, it should be added, by annal-like
descriptive references to particular events. By the time of
the Civil War, and especially in the two decades following
that conflict, another basic form evolved, which was really
an amalgamation of more specific kinds of local historical
writing that had developed separately since the 1820s.

One element in the new synthesis derived from the
genealogical compilations and group biographical sketches
that reflected the growing interest of "old" families in their
ancestral backgrounds. Another element was closely related
to the increasingly popular gazeteers, atlases, and directories,
that is, compendia of information about various communities, whether towns, cities, counties, or states. As Charles
T. Greve, in his *Centennial History of Cincinnati* (1904) put
it: "A history of a city should be neither a directory, a guide
book, nor a chronological table, and yet it is hard to avoid
giving to it some of the qualities of all these valuable methods
of treatment."[5] Still another element descended directly from
the annals and even more specialized narrative, descriptive accounts, such as the quite common military histories.

The resulting amalgamation consisted of three parts: first,
a series of chapters arranged as a narrative in a chronological sequence and focused on the early years of the community, on its settlement and initial growth; second, another series of chapters organized topically and dealing
descriptively with many different facets of the community's
life, everything from its clubs and parks and water or sewer
works to its government, its arts, and its commerce; and
third, a final, separately designed section consisting of bio-

graphical sketches of the individuals or families who were either prominent in the community or who had lived there from the beginning. This merging of families and communities—as it were—was sometimes defended in prefaces as natural and appropriate. Biographical or genealogical sketches of the old and prominent were added, in the words of an early annalist "to perpetuate their good fame, and with it, the salutary influence of their examples,"[6] or, according to a later author, "are admirably calculated to foster local ties, to inculcate patriotism, and to emphasize the rewards of industry dominated by intelligent purpose."[7]

These were the essential elements of the most mature form of nonacademic local historical writing ever developed in America. It was far more likely that the history of a city rather than the history of a town would be presented in this mold but some of the more ambitious antiquarians of smaller settlements—once again, especially in New England—put together histories that came close to matching the great variety of subjects to be found in the histories of their urban brethren.

Beginning at about the time of World War I and increasingly during the 1920s and 1930s, another form emerged: the narrative history. Sometimes written by a professional writer, often about a town or city that was widely known as distinctive or unusual in some way or other, narrative histories were presented to the general public almost as a form of travel literature. Ralph Birdsall, in his *The Story of Cooperstown* (1917), aptly summed up what such an account consisted of: "The ensuing narrative is a faithful record of life in Cooperstown from the earliest times, except that the persons and events to be described have been selected for their story-interest, to the exclusion of much that a history is expected to contain. The dull thread of village history has been followed only in such direction as served for stringing upon it and holding to the light the more shining gems of incident and personality to which it led. . . . The effort has been made to exclude everything that seemed unlikely to be of interest to the general reader."[8]

At this point, let me repeat: generalizations on this sub-

ject are risky, so varied has the enterprise under scrutiny
been, so individualistic have those involved in it been. I
cannot give you an explanation for the timing and durability
of the basic forms local historical writing has assumed since
its secularization in the early nineteenth century, any more
than I can tell you why some communities have histories
and others do not. All that I can provide is the kind of information the antiquarians themselves disclose in their prefaces as to how their books came into being. Some books[9]
started as lectures, delivered at the request of some group
and just grew into book-length treatments. Others[10] began
as edited versions of earlier histories and were turned into
new histories amalgamated with the old. Still others were
written at the invitation of town or city committees and were
presented as centennial or bicentennial histories.[11] At least
one state historical society, that of New Hampshire, appointed a Committee on Histories of the Towns.[12] During
the national centennial year of 1876, the federal government got into the act, when Congress adopted a resolution
in March, "recommending that in every town the delivery
of a historical sketch of the place from its foundation should
be part of the local celebration."[13] And, indeed, some authors
of local histories that appeared in the years following the
centennial referred to the resolution as at least partial justification for their efforts.[14] Sometimes would-be subscribers
initiated the process, with one writer admitting that the appearance of his history was "in some degree due to the solici-
tation of influential citizens."[15] Finally, several publishers
who had a special interest in producing books on local history—firms such as Lewis and S. J. Clarke—sometimes made
contracts with individuals who agreed to serve as authors or
editors for the history of certain communities.[16]

I also want to be cautious about making generalizations
concerning the identity of those who have written town and
city histories. It is clear that many were professional people
—clergymen, lawyers, doctors, journalists, politicians, authors—people with the perspective, awareness, at least some
practice as writers, and, above all, leisure time in their later
years to undertake what often was a very time-consuming

task. But others, not of this background, have presented histories because of a deep and sustained interest in their community and its past. I'm thinking particularly about women authors and scions of pioneering families. The only common denominator seems to have been age: the typical local historian has always been someone in his or her later years.

Why did they write? What motivated them? One of the earliest, Emory Washburn, summed it up rather well: "We have been prompted to this, more from feelings of local interest and attachment, than from any hope of literary reputation or, much less, of profit. The graves of our fathers are here; and we felt a curiosity to trace, not only their histories, but also those of all who were their contemporaries, and acted and suffered with them. We felt desirous of snatching from oblivion, events connected with the history of our country, and preserving the names of men whose merits deserve a place on its pages."[17] William Little said that the writing of his history "has not been a labor. It has been a pleasant pastime, a source of amusement—good fun."[18] And Silas Farmer asserted that "[time], patience, discrimination, and large expenditures of money have been essential factors in the preparation of the volume; I, however, have had no regrets, for the work has been a labor of love, and I have been increasingly glad that it was my privilege to write the history of my birthplace."[19] Perhaps the most common statement involving motivation was that the author wanted to preserve for future generations existing records and the reminiscences of pioneers before such evidence was forever lost.

What was the purpose of writing such histories? I shall again generalize, even though aware of much variety. Simply put: the pioneering or initial histories of communities in any part of the country typically were written in honor of the original settlers and constitute a record of their deeds, that is, of their successful creation of the communities their descendants inhabited. These communities were sometimes built with much hardship, whether produced by nature or by a hostile native population, and the early histories were often a celebration of pioneering hardiness, sturdiness, and persistence. In essence, this was history as a form of ancestral worship.[20] As villages grew into towns and towns into cities, later histories were typically focused on a community's growth or progress, and sometimes ended with optimistic statements concerning the future. Local history with this emphasis became a kind of "booster" literature, and its practitioners were to some extent publicity agents for fast-growing, progressive communities, whose future, it was assumed, would match their past.[21]

In sum, local history was the story of the successful, by the successful, and for the successful, an account of old-stock America—of heroic ancestors and their early settlements grown prosperous and secure through the years. Such writings provided an important means by which the durable, stable element in the American population retained a sense of place and continuity. In such a success story, there was not space for community conflict and for recent foreign immigrants. In 1855, Charles Brooks articulated what many others must have felt in one form or another when he said: "These registers of early families in New England will contain the only authentic records of the true Anglo-Saxon blood existing among us; for, if foreign immigration should pour in upon us for the next fifty years as it has for the last thirty, it will be difficult for a man to prove that he has descended from the Plymouth Pilgrims."[22] By the 1920s, writers like John M. Killits had a somewhat different reaction: "We note, perhaps with regret, that, in some parts of the country, men of alien lineage and habits of thought are taking over places hallowed with memories of early struggles in the development of our American commonwealth. . . . Wherever historical associations . . . make up local atmosphere, we may look for beneficial results when residents of any extraction are brought under their influence."[23]

Those who at first produced local histories sometimes thought of themselves as just "compilers," especially when they assembled and reproduced documents of various kinds in some sort of chronological sequence.[24] But, by the time of the Civil War, at least some writers claimed the title "historian" outright, as did Charles Hudson, when he asserted that "I could have made it [my history] more flattering; but I chose to appear in the character of a *historian*, rather than in that of a *eulogist*."[25] And, indeed, perhaps the most frequently repeated assertion in prefaces and introductions is that the author seeks to be factually accurate. There was less agreement on the desirability of trying to be impartial or objective, however. And, though doubtless all could agree in principle with Augustus Gould and Frederic Kidder who said "to 'say nothing of the dead except what is good,' is an ancient and most charitable maxim; but it is by no means one which can be admitted in impartial history,"[26] many could also appreciate Dwight Goss's comments on the difficulty of achieving impartiality.[27] It would appear that William Boyd adopted a less popular position when he stated that "it has been my intention not to give anything in this work, to reflect upon the charactor [sic] of persons, or hurt the feelings of their descendants. Should there be an instance of that kind in the book, I humbley [sic] ask their pardon from unintentionly [sic] doing them an injury."[28]

The sources local historians used varied, according to the availability of documents as well as the interest and persistence of the author. One common type of source was the oral or printed memoir, something especially common in areas west of the Appalachians where the pioneers were often still living at the time the first history was written.[29] Another often used source was the newspaper, though as I point out in another study just completed, American newspapers did not contain regular local news columns until the middle decades of the nineteenth century; this meant that, once again, the farther west a community is the more likely it is that its historians have had access to newspaper files covering the early and formative years. Large-scale city histories were also based on council records, directories, county records, state laws, federal censuses, reports of a great array of private and public organizations, annals of area historical societies, and earlier histories of the city.[30]

Though on occasion through the nineteenth century local historians referred with obvious approval to the growing popularity of town and city history,[31] the fact is that in many cases the amateur historian either supported himself while preparing his history or went after other townspeople to act as subscribers, and, indeed, some volumes contain lists of subscribers. David Noyes unashamedly told the citizens of Norway, Maine, that "should you be pleased to liberally patronize the present work, it will greatly serve to smooth the down-hill of life, which I am fast descending. . . ."[32] J. W. Hanson of Gardiner, Maine, "hopes his fellow citizens will encourage his effort by buying his book, and being pleased with it."[33] E. M. Ruttenber of Newburgh, New York, was equally candid: "Indeed, our expenditures upon the work are far in advance of the income which we have already derived from its publication, or that we may anticipate in the future."[34] Though such early writers as James Thacher of Plymouth, Massachusetts, and John Watson of Philadelphia could boast in prefaces to second editions that the first had been completely sold out,[35] the only alternative to personal expenditures or subscription guarantees for most of the amateur historians was the financial support of a town or city committee or a contract from publishers like Lewis or S. J. Clarke, who raised money from those whose biographical sketches appeared as the final section in the city histories these firms produced after the turn of the century—a practice that led critics to dub such tomes as "mug-books."

As early as 1887, the publishers of W. Scott Robison's *History of the City of Cleveland* indicated that "[in] endeavoring to profit by the experiences of the publishers of the histories of other cities, it was deemed most judicious to produce a book that could be sold at a price considerably less than that of the average local work of this kind. Voluminous and elaborate local histories, with their proportionately high cost, have not proved commercial successes. So large is the amount that one must read in these days to keep up with the times, that the majority of people find it necessary to select condensed treatments of subjects."[36] By the 1930s, condensed or shorter histories were typical, and William Bruce's defense of them was much more familiar: "The general public is not inclined to delve exhaustively into local history, . . . elaborate studies serve the research student and statesman rather than the average reader. . . . [The present volume] is intended for popular reading rather than for extensive study."[37]

Whether profitable or not, local historical writing was difficult to produce. The litany of complaints resonates through the introductory pages of hundreds of volumes like a long moan: records were scarce or incomplete; previous works were almost nonexistent; townspeople were unco-operative; the author's health was impaired; the enterprises cost too much.

With such hardship everywhere apparent, it is a tribute to the antiquarians that they, in fact, wrote so much history, especially since some of them believed that what they were doing had no value or interest to anyone beyond the inhabitants of the community they wrote about.[38] Many referred almost disparagingly to their "trivial" facts. But others argued that the collective study of particular communities provided much information on how people actually lived, in contrast to national history, which was centered on the activities of a distant federal government. Both kinds of history were important; both had value. In this way, some local historians invested their work with a significance that went beyond the preservation of the past in given towns and cities.

Others thought that such work provided its own justification, however. As Alonzo Lewis aptly put it: "There is something so natural in enquiring into the history of those who have lived before us, and particularly of those with whom we have any connexion [sic], either by the ties of relation or place, that it is surprising any one should be found by whom this subject is regarded with indifference. . . . To trace the settlement and progress of our native town—to read the history of the playplace of our early hours, and which has been the scene of our maturer joys—to follow the steps of our fathers through the course of centuries, and mark the gradation of improvement—to learn who and what they were, from whom we are descended—and still further, to be informed of the people who were here before them, and who are now vanished like a dream of childhood; and all these in their connexion [sic] with the history of the world and of man—must certainly be objects of peculiar interest to every inquisitive mind."[39] Similarly, John Watson wrote that "[our] love of antiquities—the contemplation of days by-gone is an impress of Deity.—It is our hold on immortality. The same affection which makes us reach forward and peep into futurity prompts us to travel back to the hidden events which transpired before we existed. We thus feel our span of existence prolonged even while we have the pleasure to identify ourselves with the scenes or the emotions of our forefathers."[40]

Local historical writing of the kind I've been speaking about is still being written, of course. But, as far as I am able to discern, no new forms have emerged since the development of the short narrative between the two world wars. As of now, I can only guess at the reasons for this general lack of vitality and change. Many older communities have stopped growing. The sort of people who used to write such histories —professional people—have been far more mobile in recent decades than they were in the nineteenth and early twentieth centuries and are, therefore, less rooted, have less of a sense of place. More broadly, the patterns of American life have become nationalized; little is now organized on a purely local basis; towns and cities are losing their distinctiveness, are becoming more and more alike and subjected to common national influences.

In the last decade, academic historians have become increasingly interested in the study of local communities. Indeed, university calendars now boast of whole courses on urban and rural communities. (I myself will introduce a course to be called "The Town in U.S. History" at my university next year.) This development has been sudden, and the reasons for it are not yet clear. Academic local historical writing focuses on developments affecting local communities generally, features statistical evidence that measures certain features of the lives of urban and rural populations, and is organized around concepts or models or themes, often borrowed from the social sciences. Scholars of local history shun the study of particular communities for what is unique about them, offer evidence, not interesting details, present analysis or arguments, not description or narrative, study all the inhabitants, not just prominent families, and search for common patterns in the large mosaic of rural and urban life.

What concerns me most about the dramatic entrance of academic scholars into the field of local history is that those interested in the study of the American past are now, as never before, divided into two quite separate groupings —the academic and the nonacademic. There was a common audience for national and local historical writing in the nineteenth century in the United States. The emergence of academic historical study, with its emphasis on conceptual analytical thinking, on statistical evidence, and on technical terminology, has meant that a small intelligentsia has had the means to study our history that others do not, perhaps cannot, share. And now academic history has moved into—poached upon—the territory long occupied by the amateur alone: the family and the local community. But the study of the past is too important, too fundamental, to become the preserve of specialists. What will the long-term effect for a society be when its intellectuals and its general population lose the capacity to view a common past in a common way. What dangers lurk there? I wonder. I wish I knew.

NOTES

1. On this point see Peter Gay, *A Loss of Mastery; Puritan Historians in Colonial America* (Berkeley: University of California Press, 1966).

2. Frances Caulkins, *History of Norwich* (Conn.) (Norwich: T. Robinson, 1845), p. v.

3. Samuel Swift, *History of the Town of Middlebury* (Vt.) (Middlebury: A. H. Copeland, 1859), pp. 5-6.

4. For example, Thomas W. Griffith, *Annals of Baltimore* (Baltimore: Printed by W. Wooddy, 1824); John F. Watson, *Annals of Philadelphia* (Philadelphia: E. L. Carey & A. Hart, 1830); Jacob B. Moore, *Annals of the Town of Concord* (N.H.) (Concord: J. B. Moore, 1824); and Nathaniel Adams, *Annals of Portsmouth* (N.H.) (Portsmouth: C. Norris, 1825).

5. Charles T. Greve, *Centennial History of Cincinnati* (Chicago: Biographical Publishing Co., 1904), Preface.

6. Moore, *Annals of the Town of Concord* (N.H.), Biographical Notices, p. 53.

7. William M. Rockel (ed.), *20th Century History of Springfield* (Ohio) (Chicago: Biographical Publishing Co., 1908), Preface.

8. Ralph Birdsall, *The Story of Cooperstown* (Cooperstown: The Arthur H. Crist Co., 1917), Foreword.

9. Such as John Daggett, *Sketch of the History of Attleborough* (Mass.) (Dedham, Mass.: H. Mann, printer, 1834).

10. Such as Samuel G. Drake, *The History and Antiquities of the City of Boston* (Boston: L. Stevens, 1854).

11. Such as George E. Goodrich (ed.), *The Centennial History of the Town of Dryden* (N.Y.) (Dryden: J. G. Ford, printer, 1898), or Charles Hudson, *History of the Town of Marlborough* (Mass.) (Boston: Press of T. R. Marvin & Son, 1862).

12. Charles J. Fox, *History of the Old Township of Dunstable* (N.H.) (Nashua: C. T. Gill, 1846), p. 3.

13. John S. Hittell, *A History of the City of San Francisco* (San Francisco: A. L. Bancroft & Co., 1878), p. 5.

14. See especially, W. Scott Robison (ed.), *History of the City of Cleveland* (Cleveland: Robison & Cockett, 1887), p. ix.

15. William Bache, *Historical Sketches of Bristol Borough* (Pa.) (Bristol: [W. Bache, printer], 1853), Preface.

16. There is an unusually full statement on the arrangements one author made with S. J. Clarke in Thomas W. Lewis, *Zanesville and Muskingum County, Ohio* (Chicago: S. J. Clarke Publishing Co., 1927), pp. v-vi. Another example is J. Thomas Scharf, *History of Baltimore City and County* (Philadelphia: L. H. Everts, 1881), p. vii, who said his history was "undertaken at the request of Major Lewis H. Everts, the enterprising publisher." Still another example is David L. Pierson, *History of the Oranges* (N.J.) *to 1921* (New York: Lewis Historical Publishing Co., 1922), Foreword, who comments on the role of the Lewis Publishing Company.

17. Emory Washburn, *Topographical and Historical Sketches of the Town of Leicester* (Mass.) (Worcester: Printed by Rogers & Griffin, 1826), p. 3.

18. William Little, *History of the Town of Warren* (N.H.) (Concord, N.H.: Steam Printing Works of McFarland & Jenks, 1854), pp. iii-iv.

19. Silas Farmer, *The History of Detroit and Michigan* (Detroit: S. Farmer & Co., 1884), p. v.

20. General statements concerning the character of the settlers and their villages can be found in concluding statements and, more briefly, in prefaces in various early town histories. For example: Erastus Worthington, *The History of Dedham* (Boston: Dutton and Wentworth, 1827), p. 146; James Thacher, *History of the Town of Plymouth* (Boston: Marsh, Capen & Lyon, 1835), pp. 299-300; Edwin M. Stone, *History of Beverly* (Boston: J. Munroe and Co., 1843), pp. 306-309; Herman Mann, *Historical Annals of Dedham* (Dedham,

Mass.: H. Mann, 1847), Casual Remarks, pp. 131-34; John M. Weeks, *History of Salisbury* (Vt.) (Middlebury, Vt.: A. H. Copeland, 1860), pp. 346-50.

21. Neville B. Craig, *The History of Pittsburgh* (Pittsburgh: J. H. Mellor, 1851), Chapter 15; William H. Miller, *The History of Kansas City* (Mo.) (Kansas City: Birdsall & Miller, 1881), Preface, chapters 1 and 18; Frederic J. Grant, *History of Seattle* (New York: American Publishing and Engraving Co., 1891), pp. 303-305; and William Griffith, *History of Kansas City* (Mo.) (Kansas City: Hudson-Kimberly Publishing Co., 1900), Chapter 8—contain uncharacteristically explicit statements on the nature of urban expansion. In most histories, the theme of growth and progress is implicit, something understood, but seldom directly referred to.

22. Charles Brooks, *History of the Town of Medford* (Mass.) (Boston: J. M. Usher, 1855), p. vi.

23. John M. Killits, *Toledo and Lucas County, Ohio* (Chicago and Toledo: The S. J. Clarke Publishing Co., 1923), p. iii.

24. For example: Abiel Abbot, *History of Andover* (Mass.) (Andover: Flagg and Gould, 1829), Advertisement, and Bache, *Historical Sketches of Bristol Borough* (Pa.), Preface.

25. Hudson, *History of the Town of Marlborough* (Mass.), p. viii.

26. Augustus A. Gould and Frederic Kidder, *The History of New Ipswich* (N.H.) (Boston: Gould and Lincoln, 1852), p. viii.

27. Dwight Goss, *History of Grand Rapids* (Mich.) (Chicago: C. F. Cooper & Co., 1906), Preface.

28. William P. Boyd, *History of the Town of Conesus* (N.Y.) (Conesus: Boyd's Job Printing Establishment, 1887), p. 7.

29. The more sophisticated local historians were careful to point out the distinction between such reminiscences and their own efforts, however. As Mary L. Booth put it: "It had been the fashion to tell the story of the metropolis in a series of fragmentary memoirs, full of personal reminiscences and entertaining gossip concerning leading families and familiar landmarks, but these, while affording most valuable material to the historian, were not history." *History of the City of New York* (New York: E. P. Dutton & Co., 1880), p. 3.

30. A good example is Samuel P. Orth, *A History of Cleveland, Ohio* (Chicago: The S. J. Clarke Publishing Co., 1910), pp. 8-10.

31. Early statements are those of Stone, *History of Beverly*, p. iii, and Gould and Kidder, *The History of New Ipswich* (N.H.), p. vii.

32. David Noyes, *The History of Norway* (Me.) (Norway: The author, 1852), p. v.

33. John W. Hanson, *History of Gardiner* (Me.) (Gardiner: W. Palmer, 1852), p. iv.

34. Edward Manning Ruttenber, *History of the Town of Newburgh* (N.Y.) (Newburgh: E. M. Ruttenber & Co., printers, 1859), Conclusion.

35. Thacher, *History of the Town of Plymouth*, p. iii, and John Watson, *Annals of Philadelphia* (2d ed. Philadelphia: The author, 1844), p. iii.

36. Robison (ed.), *History of the City of Cleveland*, pp. ix-x.

37. William G. Bruce, *A Short History of Milwaukee* (Milwaukee: The Bruce Publishing Co., 1936), pp. vii-viii.

38. Daggett, *Sketch of the History of Attleborough*, p. 3, made this point well.

39. Alonzo Lewis, *The History of Lynn* (Boston: Press of J. H. Eastburn, 1829), pp. 4-5.

40. Watson, *Annals of Philadelphia* (1830), p.v.

Writing Local History:

The Challenge, The Responsibilities, The Pleasure

Dorothy Weyer Creigh

Throughout the United States, local historical societies are springing up by the dozens, the hundreds. The newest directory published by the American Association for State and Local History lists something close to ten thousand historical groups, and when you translate that into numbers of members, you have an enormous body of people such as you who are enthusiastic about preserving the past and willing to devote time, energy, and talent to the job.

The basic purpose of any local historical organization is the preservation of history, whether it be through a museum which preserves and displays artifacts in creative, imaginative exhibits that interpret how people lived years ago; a society which stimulates talking about the good old days and preserves oral history; or a group which collects and preserves such archival materials as newspapers, journals, letters, photographs, and documents.

But the form in which history is most easily preserved for the ages is the written word. Old buildings may deteriorate under the ravages of the elements, arrowheads may be lost or old wedding dresses may disintegrate, and photographs, newspapers, or movie films may crumble. Stories passed from one generation to the next by oral tradition can become distorted, bearing little resemblance to actual fact after they've been repeated several times. But presumably a few copies of published books will endure for generations.

In this age of literacy, all of us are tuned to books. Whereas few of us can look at old ruins and really see the past, more can read the printed word and learn from it. There on the printed page is information we can read, and other people can read it, too—our children, our children's children.

Writing local history is one of the most challenging jobs a local historical society can undertake, and one of the most enduring. Writing it can be frustrating. It's time-consuming, costly, and permanent. For once the words are put into type and printed on the page, they're there for good. Whereas you can change exhibits, move artifacts around, put in new items, even correct a mistake on a label with little effort, that same omission or mistake on a printed page in a thousand bound books cannot be corrected easily.

Writing local history brings with it a tremendous responsibility. Both you and I know the "if it's in print, it has got to be right" syndrome. What we publish has to be correct, for our published works will be taken as gospel from now on. If we publish anything at all, it has to be absolutely accurate!

What kind of publishing do you want to do? And what kind can you afford?

Perhaps the most common type is the one-volume "History of Our Town." There are hundreds, thousands, of these books throughout the country, some of them published a hundred or more years ago, some yesterday, all of them contributing something to the body of knowledge of local history. They vary in quality from very good to horrible. They are the work of dedicated, earnest, sincere people who have worked for long periods of times, sometimes years, to put in writing something about the history of their communities. These one-volume histories are usually one-shot deals in which the authors and publishers exhaust all their facilities, their money, and their enthusiasm on single volumes.

Another kind of publishing is an historical periodical, a monthly, quarterly, or even annual magazine, which has stories on specific subjects, well-researched to be sure, each story written in more detail than could be possible if it were simply part of one book. Since this kind of publication may not be familiar to you, or since your organization may never have considered it for its own use, let me describe something about this kind of publishing first.

PERIODICALS

Many large, well-established, and well-financed groups have quarterlies, distinguished-looking magazines. These include most state historical societies and such other groups as the San Diego Historical Society having substantial financial backing. Other groups, such as the Greenbrier Historical Society in Lewisburg, West Virginia, publish annuals, each of them containing a number of well-researched stories of local history.

On the other hand, most historical groups, no matter how small, seem to publish newsletters which tell members of events of the society itself, but not of history. These publications, which I call nut cup ones, vary in size and frequency of appearance and may be mimeographed or printed. They tell about committees for the bake sale, the results of the membership drive, the forthcoming tour, or other functions of the organization. Although they are published by historical groups, they do not interpret history as such.

When our small, struggling group, the Adams County Historical Society in Hastings, Nebraska, began its modest little publishing program twelve years ago, we had no pattern to follow, for we had never seen as small a periodical as we had in mind. Within the restrictions of our infinitesimal budget, we wanted to publish a periodical about local history that was well-researched and so written as to appeal to a wide audience and to appear on a regular basis. We wanted to share our history.

With trepidation we started out a dozen years ago publishing a little four-page quarterly, an unimpressive leaflet every three months, with stories of specific happenings, events, or developments of the past. Our first stories tended to be seasonal: how Arbor Day was celebrated through the years, with much emphasis on the first ones—how townspeople gathered as a community to plant trees on the bleak prairie, how it was such an important event that the newspaper published the names of the participants and the kinds of trees they planted, how one woman lost her fur cape at the happening and had to advertise in the newspaper for it (that nugget indicating that the tree-planting must have been a social event as well as a practical one). Another story, in the fall, was about early-day football games, who organized them, coached them, played them, and where they were played, and some of the highlights from them. Other stories in those first issues were about Christmas customs of the past and about early-day summertime parades. Each story was not long, but it was on a specific subject; it was well-researched; it was on a subject that had wide appeal; and it was written in a light, happy, interesting fashion.

We had two hundred copies printed of those first little publications, and we published four issues each year. We mailed them to members (at first we were so naive that we didn't even know about bulk rates for nonprofit organizations and wasted more money than we should have on postage). But people began to read those publications. And then we could see that they were good business: we had something to offer new members of our society. People who wouldn't join our group just for the sake of joining now considered their membership a subscription to our publication. And so we began to accumulate new members. That wasn't the purpose for the publishing, of course, but it began to be an attractive dollars-and-cents supplemental reason. Before long, we began to expand.

Because of financial limitations, we are still no larger than eight pages, usually six, but we do publish twelve times a year. Our press run is two thousand copies. Our story content is more sophisticated than it was in the beginning, we go into more depth and detail, and because of our size restrictions, we often have stories which are continued from one issue to the next; in fact, several topics have been in three consecutive issues.

Some people ask, wouldn't you be better off publishing one journal a year rather than twelve little leaflets? We think not. In our particular situation, we feel that by being seen each month, we have far more visibility than we would have if our publication came out only once a year. Our publication is small in size—the kind of thing that can be read easily in a hurry—and we feel that we have a wider readership the way we are. In fact, some people have told us that our *Historical News*—what a dull title for such an intriguing little paper—is standard equipment in their bathroom libraries or bedroom nightstands. Our readers, at least, like short stories. And perhaps they would not be so receptive to longer, more time-consuming reading.

Through the years, we've noticed with much pleasure that a number of small, similarly-underfinanced local societies such as ours have borrowed our idea. One of them, the Buffalo County Historical Society in Kearney, Nebraska, intentionally copied our format almost exactly. Another, the Otter Tail County Historical Society in Fergus Falls, Minnesota, has a different format but has some of the same ideas for subject matter. I'm sure there are others.

Each of the stories in our publication is well-researched—in fact, most take from several months to several years of research before they're published. However, we want them to appeal to a wide audience, and for that reason, we do not want them to appear scholarly and pedantic. As historians, you and I know the importance of citing sources so that readers and future scholars know where information or figures came from. But you will agree that many would-be readers are completely turned off by footnotes. The little figures and dinky type at the bottom of the page scare the ordinary reader. So how do you handle your source material?

There are several ways. The Buffalo County publication lists at the bottom of each story the principal sources of information for that story. What we do is a little sneakier; whenever we can, we indicate in the body of the story where the information came from: for instance, "According to the Hastings *Tribune* of September 8, 1979, such-and-so happened," or if the information came from an interview, oral history, we say "Mrs. Harry Smith recalls that. . . ." We document the information as best we can in the story itself; then in a file folder for each story, we keep the detailed information in our archives for the use of scholars who might want more information later. And we save our raw notes, too, in those file folders, because often we aren't able to use all of the material we have collected on a given subject. For some stories which have required particularly time-consuming research in sources which might not be available to scholars generally, we also add addenda to the published stories which indicate in more detail the procedures through which we have secured data. For one particular series on the Ku Klux Klan, which took exceedingly skillful research over a period of seven years before it was ready for publication, we added a detailed account of the means by which we had collected our information.

As a scholar, I grieve that we do not fully document our stories as they appear, but as a practical person, I know that we gain in audience by not using the usual footnote format. We hope that we are striking a happy medium so that scholars can follow our sources.

What kinds of subjects do we cover? A wide variety, covering a wide period of time. Because our audience spans a wide difference in age and interests, we try to have some which are purely nostalgic to appeal to people who have long since moved away, some for high school-aged boys, some for farmers still on the land, some for motherly types, some for townspeople who have recently moved into the area. If one story is about the development of arts in the area, focusing particularly on the 1880s, for instance, then the next one will be on baseball in the 1920s, to provide variety and interest for a different audience.

Some of the stories are one-shot deals. For instance, in 1915, the Liberty Bell was put on a flatcar and pulled around the United States so that people all over the country could see it. We researched old newspapers, found the accounts of when the Liberty Bell came to our town, and then interviewed the people who were still living and got their accounts and borrowed their pictures. It was a great story for the Bicentennial Year of 1976. In fact, it was reprinted in the *Magazine of the Midlands* and the *Congressional Record*.

We did a light-hearted series of stories on bootlegging and prohibition, starting with the beginning of the prohibition movement in the 1870s and carrying it through, issue after issue, to national prohibition, bootlegging, and on to repeal. How we accumulated that material is an hilarious yarn in itself, and for that series, we had to be particularly evasive about naming our sources. (That source file, by the way, is sealed in our archives and cannot be opened until 2000.) Youngsters particularly seemed to enjoy reading about that phase of history; apparently their history books do not handle it as a subject involving people.

We've done stories on ethnic groups—the French-Canadians, the Germans from Russia, and the Irish. We did a story on the Black Masonic lodge, on the flu epidemic of 1918-1919, and on the rise and fall of wide-spot-in-the-road communities. We've done specific ones on the Dust Bowl years and on industries. One of my favorites was a poignant one, based on an old letter which a young father wrote in 1890 at the time his two-year-old baby daughter died of croup. We've had stories about barber shops and beauty shops and how they've changed, of ice cream parlors and of brickyards. One which attracted much favorable comment was simply called "The Sounds of the Town" which evoked much nostalgia; another was "The Smells of Christmas," focusing on candle wax, green trees, and ethnic Christmas cooking. We try to recreate in our writing an age long gone. The subject matter is unlimited.

Who writes the stories? Anybody who wants to, but the stories must be carefully edited, researched, and documented and written in a light, happy, easy-to-read style. We call our style spritely, but it is not smart-alecky. We do not want dull stories. For too long American history was a dreary classroom subject of dates and names of presidents. We want interesting social history, which we call our material to show how people lived, what they did and why, what made them tick. We want the past to come alive through our stories.

A veterinarian suggested a series of stories about early-day horse doctors and how veterinary science has changed. We assigned him the job and he learned to do careful research. He was astonished at how much time it took, too; it was two years before he had all his material amassed. His manuscript was mostly rewritten to get it into an interesting style. A housewife wrote a Christmas story about a doll that had been in her family for many generations; another wrote about the gypsies that used to be around every summer. A woman of Irish descent did the research for that story. Whenever the stories are rewritten—and many of them have to be, to pass our definition of spritely—the person who does the rewriting works carefully with the researcher to make sure that the interpretations and nuances are retained in the new version.

If you have newspaper reporters or English teachers who are interested in history, try to get them interested in writing for your publication. Anyone capable of writing easily and willing to take the time for the necessary careful, detailed research is a good potential contributor. A banker in our town who was a college sports editor is enjoying researching and writing the history of football, baseball, track, and horse racing events; a former farm editor is tracing the history of irrigation. These and others who have assignments from us have been charged with the absolute need for total accuracy, for they too realize that whatever is printed is permanent; future scholars will consider our publications as accurate source material. The Adams County group usually has from five to seven stories in progress at any given time— researchers writing and calling for information and searching records for accurate information on the assigned subject. The writing of history cannot be tossed off lightly; it is better to miss a deadline than to include a fact or figure that you cannot document.

Where do you get the material? I've suggested some sources. Old newspapers are an obvious and usually a good source. If your own local historical society or your newspaper office does not have files of newspapers or microfilms of them, then read them at your state historical society. Interviews with old-timers, through the medium of oral history, will help fill in details, but make sure you realize the pitfalls of recollections; when you interview, try to have frames of reference against which you can judge the accuracy of the reminiscences. In our town we have an eighty-eight-year-old man whose memory is phenomenal. Although we still check dates and locations and other information he gives us against documentary evidence, we have never found him to be in error; he is a beautiful shining exception to the rule that you must always take at face value the recollections of old-timers.

Old, previously published volumes of local history are all right as a starting point for your own research but whenever you can, go back to original sources. You don't want to perpetuate any historical errata of the past. Use original records. The county courthouse has such records as marriage licenses —we had to use some of that material for a series of stories on how wedding customs on the prairie have changed through the years. The courthouse also has abstracts of deeds showing ownership of real estate and tax records. Sheriffs' records are another source—we had to use both sheriff and police records for our series of stories on bootlegging, and I thought I'd never get out of the police station, for the men on duty kept coming to the desk where I was working and reading over my shoulder! In our state, the county treasurer issues automobile licenses—and we needed such information for a series we did on early automobiles.

The city hall has records. The death books, for instance, were useful when we needed information for the stories on the flu epidemic and medical practices, especially one on the placards the town physician used to nail on the door when somebody had measles or scarlet fever.

There are federal records, too—the census records I'm sure you all know about. If you're doing anything about ethnic groups, you'll have to use census tables which show countries of origin—how many people living in your county in a given decade came from Germany, from Ireland, from Sweden. There are agricultural census records, and other special census records, such as businesses and minerals, a vast body of information available in figures from the U. S. Commerce Department. Then there are state and federal records about community activities, such as WPA-type projects.

Use old scrapbooks when you can. We did a series of

stories on dancing schools and borrowed scrapbooks to look at the programs from dance recitals. Some school annuals and church bulletins will have information.

Sometimes you'll need encyclopedias for general background information. When I did a series of stories on the sugar beet workers, I needed to know about sugar beet culture generally, and the *Britannica* provided the information nicely. It was also helpful when I did a story on the Jerusalem artichoke, a kind of sunflower that was grown in our area during the Dust Bowl years.

Your information will come from many, many different sources, places you probably have never thought of before. Use your imagination. Ask yourself—what do I need to know about this particular subject? where can I get the information? Perhaps one source will suggest another. Take all the time you need to be sure you have exhausted all possible sources for factual material before you start to write.

Many of the stories in our Adams County publication are in the works for a year or more before they go into print; it takes a long time to verify and corroborate research. But it is worth the wait to know that you have followed all possible avenues to search out information relative to the story content and verified every bit of information; the story is now as accurate as possible.

One of the most helpful tools to researchers these days is the copying machine, available in libraries, courthouses, almost everywhere. If you can copy directly from the original document or newspaper story, you'll have the material exactly as it appeared originally and you won't run the risk of transposing the figures, misspelling, or making some other kind of mistake. The invention of the photocopying machine is one of the biggest boons to historians ever. Hopefully, this development will prevent contemporary historians from making some of the silly errors that their predecessors have inadvertently put into print.

After our little publication had been going for almost three years—and some of our readers said they'd lost copies of this issue or given away that one—we decided to put the stories into more permanent form. That's what local historical societies are all about—preserving the past.

Just as the photocopying machine helps historians, so, too, does offset printing. We had had the printer save the negatives and plates from our little periodicals, and now at the end of every three years we gather that material together and publish the stories in a paperback book. The type is already set, the photographs are on halftone negatives, and the labor charges therefore are minimal since much of the work is already done. And as a result we have paperback book collections of our stories in a more permanent form than in the little leaflet version. The page size of the book is the same as that of our periodical. Our first volume was a collection of stories reprinted exactly as they had appeared originally.

In the second, third, and fourth volumes, however, we found it necessary to expand the original stories. As we have gained expertise, so have our readers grown in sophistication, and it often happens that after a story appears in its original form, some of our readers will come up with supplemental data or pictures of which we'd had no knowledge when we wrote the story the first time. We can expand and enlarge the stories when they appear in the book—and that's a plus for historical accuracy, and also, incidentally a good selling point when we put the books on the market. Occasionally some of the expanded stories turn out to be twice as long with twice as many pictures as there were in their original form. This is the only time, really, when the writer of a local history has a chance to add newly-discovered material, clarify an interpretation, or even correct a misprint.

How do we finance this publishing program? There are several ways. One is paying the cost of producing monthly publications out of membership fees. Many out-of-town members of historical organizations consider their membership fees to be subscriptions. If you have a publishing program in connection with your society, do not overlook the use of high school alumni lists for possible new members when you are in the midst of a membership campaign; persons who have moved away from their old hometown are often more nostalgic, more eager to read about the days they remember than are those who have stayed in town.

Another means of financing a publishing program is to ask for help from the business community. The Otter Tail County Historical Society, for instance, had its quarterly published through funding from the local power company; each issue had the notation in small type that the printing of this issue was financed by the Otter Tail Power Company. That was a quiet, low-key ad for the power company and a benefit to the historical society. The Adams County group has each issue paid for by a separate company, a small line on the second page indicating that this issue is sponsored by the First National Bank, or a lumber yard, a bottling company, an irrigation company, or a department store. In soliciting for that money, the historical society asks for enough to cover not only the printing costs but also the mailing costs of the publication. If you do "go commercial," that is, acknowledge funding from outside sources for your publication, do not allow distracting, hard-sell advertisements on your pages, but keep the commercials small and discreet. Yours is an historical publication, not an advertising medium.

The Buffalo County Historical Society paid for its first year's publishing costs through a grant from the Nebraska Committee for the Humanities and gained so many memberships from it, that from then on it was able to pay its printing costs out of its newly-expanded membership coffers.

Some organizations are interested in occasional publications, the printing of booklets about specific subjects or geographic areas within their boundaries: the story of George Rogers Clark, published by the Vincennes (Indiana) Historical and Antiquarian Society; the story of certain aspects of Puritan society published by the Pilgrim Society of Plymouth, Massachusetts; an account of covered bridges, published by a Pennsylvania historical group; even children's drawing books published by various societies to give a scaled-down, basic history of a specific region. Included among these, too, are brochures printed as guides to historic houses. These pamphlets or booklets are not published as periodicals, on a regular schedule, nor are they the magnum opus of the History of Our Town published once-in-a-lifetime. But perhaps there will be some ideas among those presented for the publishing of a single large-scale work to which you can apply your publishing programs.

BOOKS

Many historical groups are interested in compiling detailed histories of their own area to be printed in book form. Sometimes these are planned to coincide with an anniversary— the centennial, bicentennial, or some other significant occasion of a town or region; others are planned simply because the group appreciates the need for putting into type the history which it is preserving.

Many of the procedures I've told you about earlier apply to publishing books. The first and most important concern is, of course, accuracy. And in the printing of large-scale books, accuracy is even more important than in periodicals. For what is on the printed page of a book is taken as the truth from then on; if it's in print, it must be right. Your responsibility is to see that it *is* right, accurate. Check and double-check, and then check again.

Once in a while, you'll find diverse accounts of a single happening. A case in point concerns the Blizzard of 1888 in Adams County, Nebraska. One of the word-of-mouth legends in our community said that one country schoolteacher stretched a rope from the schoolhouse to the house across the road and that she had youngsters hang onto the rope to get to safety overnight in the house. The legend had been told so many times that we accepted it as fact. But while we were researching information for something else in old newspapers, in the letters to the editor column in a January 15, 1906, newspaper, we found an entirely different account. The teacher herself wrote what had gone on: early in the storm she had sent the boys out to the coal pile to bring in coal and she assigned them to keep the stove fired up all night long, had the children play active games through the night to keep warm, and had kept them in the building until the storm abated. Her letter also said that the school board had raised ned* with her afterward because she had let some children play cards—that was a sin, you know—and they docked her a day's wages because she didn't hold school the next day. The word of mouth legend, which everyone for years had accepted as true, turned out to have been changed somehow along the way. I felt that the story which the teacher herself told eighteen years later was more likely to be the accurate version than the one repeated ninety years later. (If we had had a copy of somebody's diary, written at the time, it might have contained other details which have long-since been lost.)

How did we handle this situation? Because the word of mouth legend was so commonly repeated, we printed it, terming it a legend, and then gave the story from the newspaper, much as I've told it to you here but in more detail, and let the readers decide which version they wished to accept. A weaselly solution to a problem, you may say, but we felt it let our readers in on some of the problems of historical research! Certainly this whole account in itself is not important in overall history, but it does indicate some of the problems facing an historian as he goes about his research.

Your first responsibility as an historian is accuracy. Use every resource at your command to insure that what you write and publish is accurate. As I said, if it's in print your readers have a right to assume that it must be true.

Your second responsibility is the organization of your book. All too often I have seen well-meaning efforts at local history turn out to be mish-mash collections, unrelated essays, personal accounts, all mixed together in confusion. Your book must have some kind of organization.

There are several ways of organizing your book, and no single one is preferable to any other. In fact, you may be well-advised to combine several different forms to develop

* Old ned is a nickname for the devil.

an organization which is peculiarly suited to your own circumstance.

One is chronological, the account of your town starting with its organization and telling what happened, step-by-step, after that. In fact, no matter what kind of outline or organization you follow, you must present your work chronologically to show cause-and-effect relationships in the development of the community: because this happened, something else could take place later, or conversely, this happened as a result of an event ten or fifty years ago. The big disadvantage to a strictly chronological type of organization is that in the effort to document everything of importance in a given era, it is often difficult to give enough emphasis to the really significant events, and the book has a tendency to be superficial because there isn't enough space to concentrate on events that deserve considerable elaboration. A book which is organized on a chronological basis often becomes simply a listing of events with no effort at interpreting or assessing them.

Another form is that of topical organization, in which the writer takes one topic and follows it through—the development of the city government, for instance, and chapters on the development of schools, churches, business, and industry. There are interrelationships between topics; these, too, you must show, along with cause-and-effect relationships and the development of whatever subject you are writing about.

The best form is one which combines, somehow, both the topical and chronological approach. I am not saying the form we chose for the big fat Adams County book is better than any other, but it seems to have worked out reasonably well for us. (Our book, by the way, won the Award of Merit from the American Association for State and Local History.) The first third of our 1,200-page book is a chronological account of the development of the community, from the first settlers onward. We described the terrain and what was going on in the United States at that time, and then told why it was that this area was settled. We set the stage. Then we gave a chronological account of the big, general happenings that occurred as the area developed—how the county government was established, businesses and services came along, and changes occurred. We divided the chapters by decades—not a logical division, because people don't march along in so neat a pattern—but so that at the end of each chapter, we could use U. S. census figures to show how the county had grown—or in some cases, had not grown—every ten years.

The last two thirds of our book is divided into topical chapters, detailing some of the broad general subjects in the chronological account. One chapter is on the people— who they were, where they came from and why, what they did and how they lived. Because the settlement of our part of the country was influenced by the late-1880 immigration from northern Europe, we studied immigration patterns and went into some detail to show how German and Czech and Irish cultures influenced the development of our town. Other chapters are on schools, churches, business and industry, agriculture, and so on, with broad general information given first and then specifics. Because we assumed that our book would serve partly as a reference book, we were careful to include exact dates, places, names, all of the strictly historical data that are necessary, but we included an interpretation of that material as well.

Whatever form you choose, the first step in implementing it is to read over all of the newspapers that were ever published in your area, and to read them in sequence. This is an horrendous job, I assure you. But only through a careful chronological reading of the newspapers to see what happened can you have a feeling of the past. Learn how outside influences affected your community—how did the Spanish-American War affect it? or crop failures? or the railroad strike of the 1890s? or the coal strike at the end of World War I? or the depression of the 1930s? or World War II? Remember that your community is not an island—it was and is affected by what goes on in the outside world, the happenings in the rest of the state, the nation, and even the world. Set your community in context.

Then, too, remember that history has gone on for all the years your community has been organized. A common fault of many local histories is that they focus on the early years and completely overlook the happenings of fifty, thirty, even ten years ago. It's a big temptation to dwell on the earliest years. They were so long ago, and the stories are so much different from what's happening now that they are more dramatic than are the events all remember. But you are publishing your book for generations to come and they need to know about the "in-between" years and the "now" years as well as the early years. The hardest part of writing local history is assessing the now years. The more recent the event, the more difficult it is to put it into perspective. For instance, when I wrote the Adams County book, it was at a time that college students were in revolt on the campus; I still remember how I pondered and tried to figure out how important those activities would later prove to have been!

Also remember that your book is to represent the whole community, not just the people in the big Victorian houses on the hill, but the mill workers, the domestic workers, the hired farmhands who have also been an integral part of the community. It's often more difficult to unearth information about the little people than it is the business leaders, the wheelers-and-dealers in the community, but they, too, have influenced the development of the town and are part of the total history.

Why bother to read all of the newspapers, you say, just for the sake of reading them? I call it the total immersion principle and say that to understand an era, you must absorb so much information about it that you feel as though you were living in it yourself. You must be able to react to circumstances in the way you would have at that time. For instance, when I was researching the period of the 1930s, the Dust Bowl era in Nebraska, for ten or twelve hours a day, I read the newspapers in sequence, and one day when I came out of the library, I thought, "Look at all that green grass!" I expected to see a sky full of dust and grit and heat waves!

One of the many values about reading every issue of the newspaper is that you can read between the lines to find little clues to social history. What effect did the advent of crystal radio sets or television have on your community? There are no stories to describe those events as they happened, of course, but there may be a story about how some youngster in your town heard San Francisco on his crystal set last night and that will give you a hint as to how important radio was as a social instrument. Or a story about how people tattooed their chickens may give you an idea about chicken stealing and about times in general. The newspaper won't say in so many words that times are rough, but if you know that chicken stealing is more common than it was, then you have a clue. An historian has to be part detective. Part of your story should be social history—how people lived in the 1920s, 1930s, 1940s, and on up to the present, as well as in the earliest years of the community.

Remember too that the sin of omission is as bad as that of commission. According to early-day histories of our town, there was no evil; the town was a lily-white one of church-going souls. But in reading the newspapers, I discovered that the early histories had committed sins of omission in not mentioning the seamier side of a rough, frontier community. We did not want our book to be a police gazette-type publication, but we feel that it reflects fairly and accurately the total life of the community, insofar as we can determine what it was at the time; it mentions saloons, gambling, and houses of pleasure.

The total effect of your book should be to describe each era or period as it happened, and how that era affected the ones that followed. The things that are going on today, as you well know, are based on what happened yesterday. You need interstate highways now because automobiles are common; you must mention something about the development of the automobile age, the first cars in your town, the first garages and gas stations, and the development of dependency upon cars.

How do you handle controversial issues? In almost every community there have been heated, emotionally-charged events which have divided the town. If they are of real significance, the historian has the obligation to write of them, taking a balanced, unbiased view, pointing out the varying opinions and reactions to them. If your town had newspapers with opposing views at that time, study all newspapers carefully. If lawsuits were involved, study the legal findings. As an historian, you cannot take sides, but you must report the event fairly and impartially. If the event involves people still living or happenings in the not-too-distant past, you would be wise to have several people of opposing opinions read what you have written to assure that you have not unwittingly, perhaps, made a less-than-impartial assessment of the event.

Who is to write your history? People who are completely dedicated to the job, willing to spend all their waking hours on it for months and months. It is a solitary, time-consuming job. You will have committees and delegate responsibility and authority to others, but in the end, if your book is to be a comprehensive, cohesive one, it will be the work primarily of one person who will co-ordinate the whole effort, editing and probably writing all of it.

You will have a committee structure to work out the organization of the book—the details of financing, merchandising, and all the non-editorial chores. There will be researchers who will do much of the legwork—gathering records and statistical information—as well as picture-gatherers to collect photographs (as you know, photographs tell stories better than words). But in the long run, the book will be the work of one dedicated person, whether he is the farmer from Osceola, Nebraska, who spent three years writing the history of Polk County, or the retired teacher in Morgantown, West Virginia, who did Kanawha County, or any of the other long-suffering people all over the country who have produced local histories. Be sure the author's name is on the book. Although you will give credit, of course, to everybody who helped in any way in its production, make sure that the name of the writer (i.e., the principal person involved in production), is on the cover and on the title page of the book.

Among the auxiliary crews, assign one person or group to gather information about schools, another about churches, a third for business and industry. Have someone follow cultural activities and the arts, including folk arts, and all other facets of your town. The various subjects you will want to cover in your book will include even the weather, the climate, and storms which have had an effect on your community.

Your researchers can use form letters to start to gather information. The group which works on schools, for instance, can develop a list of the basic information they need to know about each school: name, date of organization, numbers of grades at first, numbers of students through the years, names of teachers, administrators, school board members, courses taught, descriptions and locations of school buildings, and any other significant highlights. That group should ask for copies of any booklets, pamphlets, or other materials available; in the case of schools, these could include school papers, PTA yearbooks, annuals, and school board meeting minutes. Even financial reports have interesting items in them: comparative salaries for teachers through the years, comparative costs of books, fuel, supplies, and differences in qualifications for teachers.

Other groups of researchers will follow the same procedures for churches, organizations, businesses, and other sections of your book. Figure out what you need to know about each subject and compose a form letter to ask for that information. Set a deadline for the return of those questionnaires; when most of them don't show up on time, go out and get them. You and your researchers will learn to nag.

The people who are collecting photographs must have specific instructions as well. Most of the pictures will be merely loaned to you; they may come from prized family scrapbooks. Be sure that every photograph you collect is properly and inconspicuously labeled—telling what the picture is about, who the people are from left to right (give exact names, not Uncle George and Aunt Sophie, but Mr. and Mrs. George Zilch), the location, the event, the date as closely as you can pinpoint it. Add the name and address of the person who loaned it to you. Make sure the donors understand that it may be months, even a year or two, before you can return the pictures to them. Ideally, you'd have copies made of those pictures before you return them to keep in your own archives, but unfortunately, few local historical societies seem to have enough money for that. When you write the captions for the book, indicate the source of the pictures: "Photo courtesy George Zilch." The line will make him feel important, as he should, and will tell you where you can borrow the photo again, if necessary.

The writing of local history can be a community enterprise. The more people who have had a hand in collecting information, the more enthusiasm you'll generate about it. Place stories in your local newspapers about what you are doing, get in touch with secretaries of organizations, know where church and school records are kept, get acquainted with people in the courthouse, and before long, you'll be in a jungle of raw source material, astonished at all the information that will be flowing in. Be sure you indicate the source of each bit of information.

Your book will indicate sources—perhaps not by footnotes for the same reasons as we discussed before. But you should have a detailed section of notes at the end of each chapter or at the end of the book itself. This book will be the definitive history of your town. If you don't want to have regular footnote numbering, you can indicate page and line numbers and give the source of that information. For instance, in the notes at the end of this big fat book, the notes read as follows: in Chapter 3, "page 19, lines 9 and 10, lease-form in possession of Mrs. G. Paul Charlton"; paragraph 2, from Janet Carpenter speech, April 19, 1939, given at Hastings College chapel program." This gives future scholars the source of that information.

Your researchers have gathered all of the information you will need, and your editor or general writer—your "number one" person—will put it all together. It will be cohesive, logical, interesting; it will not be a hodgepodge of separate unrelated stories. It will show cause-and-effect relationships; it will indicate how people lived, how they dressed, and what their homes were like, even something of their thought processes at given periods of time. Why did they react as they did? It will be more than just a compilation of statistics and facts—those are for World Almanacs, not local histories. It will be an interpretation.

One very important subject I haven't mentioned yet is how to choose a printer. Your choice of printer for the local history book is important since the job is a big one, and the book you produce will serve as the history of your community for a long period of time; in many cases, it's fifty or more years between publication of local history volumes. You will want a book that will be worthy graphically of your efforts—an attractive, appealing book. Do not scrimp in the printing of your book.

If there is no printer available locally to handle the job—and book printing is a special art—make inquiries from the state historical society and other organizations which have had recent publishing experience. Ask them whom they have used for printing and whom they would recommend; also ask them whom they do not recommend—sometimes that's even more important! Ask about the quality of work each of the printers turns out, the reliability of each, and adherence to deadlines. One local historical society discovered midway through the production of its book that the printer, a student-operated shop which was part of a technical college, was going out of business. The society had to scurry around to find someone else to finish the job, causing a delay of almost a year and resulting in two different kinds of typeface and a book whose total appearance is not commensurate with the editorial quality of the volume. Other groups have experienced unbelievable delays in printing. Find out all you can about various printers before you ask them for bids so that you need not bother with those whom you believe are obviously not the ones you will want to work with.

When you know what printers you will want to consider, talk to them even before you ask for bids. See what kind of technical help they will be able to give. Do they have good designers on the staff, and will they work closely with you?

Ask to see some of their work; do the books have sufficient white space on the pages, enough blank pages in the front and back sections to set them off? Is the typeface readable and is the display type in the chapter headings and beginning pages compatible with the typeface? How much help will they give you making layouts? Will they work willingly with you and take pride in the book or will they merely consider this another job to crank out between others? As you look at samples of other books they have printed, talk to persons responsible for those books to see if they have been satisfied with the service they have had.

When you get to the point of asking for bids or estimates from printers, make sure that all the estimates are based on the same terms and qualifications so that your comparisons are accurate. These estimates should include: the cost of typesetting, page makeup, printing; the number of copies; the page size, type size, paper quality; pictorial content and the screen or quality of pictures (the higher the number of lines in the screen, the finer the quality of reproduction, and the higher the cost); and a clear definition of responsibilities. Does the printer read proof or do you? Does he make the dummy layout or do you? Does he arrange for binding, and will it be soft-cover or hardbound? If it is soft-cover, what kind of gluing or stitching; if it is hardbound, will it have headbands (extra stitching glued in for durability) and what will be the weight of the boards, the quality of buckram? Will you have a dust jacket? Who designs it? What quality of paper? What guarantee do you have about delivery date?

If you are obligated by law to accept the lowest bid, be especially sure that the estimate sheets cover every possible contingency; many low bidders are low simply because the estimator is figuring the cheapest quality and not including professional services the customer has every right to expect from a printer.

When you draw up a contract with the printer, be sure all these items are written in so that you will not end up with inferior paper quality or some other substitution that will dismay you. Deadlines should be clearly stated, both for the delivery of copy from you and for the delivery of the printed, finished volume. Do not rush the task of selecting and negotiating with your printer. The job he does will stay on the bookshelf for a long time.

You want to be sure that the manuscript is complete in all details, neatly typed and double-spaced, before you turn it in to the typesetter, and that it is marked according to the printer's instructions so that there are no ambiguities in direction. Changes cost money.

After the manuscript is at the printshop, you must begin one of the most important parts of the book—the index. An historical volume, especially, is no better than its index because that is the reference your readers and scholars need to locate the information they want.

The printer sets the manuscript into type, then makes proofs which are read and corrected, and finally puts the type into page form. The pages are arranged in segments called signatures, which may be eight, sixteen, or thirty-two pages in size, depending on press and page sizes, with each page numbered as it will be in the book. Ask the printer to make two proofs of each signature, one for you to make a last-minute check—to make sure that pictures are turned right side around, that the proper pictures are on each page, that the corrections you indicated in the proof have indeed been made, and that everything is exactly as you want it in the finished book. Check it over carefully, marking any necessary corrections, initial it, and return it to the printer. You will use the second copy to compile your index.

Possibly the easiest way to read the book for indexing purposes is to use a ruler so that you can read the page line by line, making notations on a ruled sheet of paper about the information in each line of the book. Say that your copy mentions Sunday movies.

One entry might be "Jones, Harry A., city councilman, stand on Sunday movies, 1913, p. 374."

Another entry for that same subject could be "Sunday movies, stand of Harry A. Jones, councilman, 1913, p. 374."

A third could be "Movie, Sunday, stand of Harry A. Jones, councilman, 1913, p. 374."

Still another could be "Recreation: see Movies"—all of these entries for one small item of information on one page of the book. The more information you have in your index, the more valuable it will be to researchers and scholars. A name with no other information about it is annoying, and a general subject-topic is likewise of little help. Be generous in your indexing, and try to put yourself in the place of a scholar fifty years from now who is looking for information. What subjects would you look under?

In addition to general entries, you will want cross-references. For instance, under "Schools," you may want to make "also see" entries, such as "see athletics" or "see music" or "see population" for entries in those classifications that have relevance to the general subject of schools. The more detail you have, the more useful the index; rather than saying "Irrigation, p. 238," it is far more useful to say "Irrigation, public meeting about legal problems, 1967, p. 238."

If you have time for more than one person to index each signature, you will have a double check on entries for the index; even when indexes are prepared by professional index compilers they often are not detailed enough. Librarians, teachers who have had library science courses in cataloging, and persons who have done considerable research and know from experience what general topics they look for, are likely candidates for volunteer help in preparing your index. Indexing is sometimes tedious but it is essential to any volume on local history. Allow plenty of time for it. After the listings have been made on lined paper, have volunteer typists prepare cards, one entry to a card, and file the cards alphabetically.

Finally, weeks after all the signatures of the book have been combed for index entries and all cards have been alphabetized, it is time to compile the index as it should be for the printer. One historical society had an Index-Typing Day, gathering twenty typists in a large office room, each typist taking a separate letter of the alphabet, one person typing the A's, another the B's, and so on. With twenty persons working together, the whole typing procedure took four hours of time, and the occasion was one in which those people could share the labor and make their own contribution to the book. What could have been drudgery for one was a sociable experience for many.

How do you finance your book?

The books we have been talking about here are not those which have biographical entries in them, the sort of Who's Who volumes that local historical organizations sometimes publish. Those are valuable as reference books, particularly for genealogists, but they are not really histories and should not be so considered. Some commercial organizations which compile volumes such as these charge for entries; in the past, there were many printers who made a living publishing such books for counties or towns.

The financing of a local history book has to come from other sources. And the costs of printing a detailed local history are usually far greater than any amount that an ordinary historical society can save up over the years. The group must make special arrangements for financing such an undertaking.

One way is prepublication sales. How do you figure the selling price of a book so that you can take orders before publication? You must determine the total cost of the book, bound and delivered to you and ready for distribution, plus whatever advertising costs you will have, including posters, newspaper advertisements, flyers and promotional materials, and other costs associated with the distribution of the book. Divide this total figure by the number of books you are having printed, and you will arrive at the actual cost per book. Then multiply that actual cost per book by three to reach the lowest possible cost you can afford as the selling cost of the book.

Why multiply by three? There are several reasons: you certainly will not sell all the books immediately (in fact, if you do, you've not ordered enough; you should order enough so that you will have a few left for the orders that may dribble in ten, fifteen, even twenty years later), but you will have to pay the printer's bill right away; you will have to send out an alarming number of "freebies," two to the Library of Congress to establish your copyright, several to book reviewers in local, regional, or state newspapers, to your state historical society, and others as courtesy copies, perhaps to the governor and state and federal lawmaking representatives, among others; if you turn over some book sales to bookshops or book brokers, you will have to allow them sufficient discount that they are interested in handling them. For these reasons especially, you simply cannot establish your lowest selling price at any less than three times actual cost. Use this as your prepublication price for persons who are willing to order the book early. Establish your regular selling price at a figure enough above that that persons will find it advantageous to order early, paying for the books upon delivery.

Unless you are unusually fortunate in your prepublication sales, however, you still will need outside funding to pay the printer's bill. Before you begin the writing of the history, find out what alternative funding is available—perhaps through the Chamber of Commerce and local business firms; through city or county funds, a source that grows less likely by the year; through revenue-sharing funds, if they continue to be available; through foundation support; through whatever means you can conjure up. You will undoubtedly have to resort to a combination of funding sources to be able to finance the publication of your detailed, exceedingly valuable book on the History of Your Town.

I shall not begin to enumerate here ways and means of merchandising your book. They are covered in some detail in the chapter on publishing in *A Primer for the Local Historical Society,* published by the American Association for State and Local History, and I'm sure you can add your own suggestions to the ones there. What I hope I have been able to give you here has been some concrete help about the organizing, writing, and publishing of your local history which will be useful to your local historical organization.

The publishing of local history should be a significant consideration for any local historical group; it really does preserve history, fulfilling the prime purpose of all historical societies. To publish is a challenge, with responsibilities galore, but all of you who do undertake a publishing program will soon agree that it brings with it even more pleasure and satisfaction. I wish you well.

Humanities and the Study of Local History

Roger Fortin

I read recently that all is not well in history classrooms. Too often, it appears that history is being taught by inadequately trained teachers. The courses are too narrow and factual, lacking in enthusiasm and imagination. On a related note, how are museums, historic sites, and community studies faring? Is history being taught by inadequately trained interpreters? Do they possess enthusiasm and imagination? Are museum tours and historical exhibits too narrow and factual?

In my judgment, the approach we take in examining the American past is all-important. The interpreter cannot teach or speak intelligibly about history apart from the humanities. The humanities deal with that which is distinctively human in the lives of people in society—their many institutions, beliefs, and culture. When properly studied, they illustrate the depth and scope of human thoughts and feelings and the imaginative ways in which peoples' thoughts and values are expressed.

Indeed, individuals who interpret the humanities wish to come to grips with the vitality and essence of society. They show the functions and relationships of people in their environment and evaluate certain basic beliefs which guide human lives. They may want to show what it was like to live before automobiles, airplanes, electric dryers, television, and radio, to cook without gas or electric stoves, and to read by candlelight. They may want to show what it meant years ago being part of a family, working in a New England factory, attending a one-room schoolhouse, living in a Shaker community, being in bondage, earning a comfortable living, or building a community. By studying peoples' ideas and surviving artifacts—their houses, furnishings, and landscape—we get to know what sort of people they were, what they did in their everyday lives. We must never lose our collective memory.

Significantly, too, a basic assumption is made about the study and interpretation of history. It is assumed that when people understand how other people lived, understand how some were betrayed by greed and hate, and others were rewarded through hard work, personal sacrifice, or good fortune, they are more likely to lead lives which characterize them at their best as human beings.

To be sure, community studies and interpretations at museums and historic sites should place the accent on humanity and encourage the consideration of values. And the sponsors of community educational programs should proceed delicately and with great care in the interpretation of America's legacy. They are the guardians of a cultural heritage, the beneficiaries of a rich tradition. Precious deposits of America's past are for their keeping and interpretation. As William T. Alderson and Shirley Payne Low point out in their publication, *Interpretation of Historic Sites*, the responsibilities associated with the concept of guardianship should not be taken lightly. "Our trusteeship places upon us," they argue, "an ethical commitment to accuracy in restoration, truth in interpretation, and protection for the next generation."

Doubtlessly, history as a discipline is pivotal to a study of the past. It provides a dimension of human life. It reflects the diversities of human experience: people playing, working, dancing, grieving, embracing, creating, and worshiping. But historians are not the only people who visit the past. Increasingly, scholars are identifying more and more disciplines, ranging from history and economics to cultural geography and archaeology, from which you may draw their humanistic character, their capacity to deal with human experiences. To be sure, the study of history comes in many varieties, and each discipline has its own pursuits and provides unique insights into past culture and events.

Before I discuss varied approaches to a study of man's past culture, I would like to underline an essential point. Interpreters of history have a professional responsibility to establish as accurate an account of the past as our knowledge and critique of documents and artifacts will permit. We must always edit documents responsibly and critically in order to ascertain their credibility. For example, upon examination of the customs of a people, our information should be carefully tested for authenticity, distinguishing fact from legend.

However, once we collect relevant evidence and arrive at some reliable statement on objects or events in a community, interpreters should not profess certainty as to order and movement in history. The historian's faith, wrote the late Charles Beard, "is at bottom a conviction that something true can be known" about them. And as the historian considers things in process of development, "any selection and arrangement" of written materials and artifacts "pertaining to any area of history" is controlled inexorably by the frame of reference in his mind. What also influences the writing and interpreting of history is the contemporary climate of opinion and interest. Each generation of historians reworks history from new points of view. The interpreter's angle of vision changes. And if we are allowed one certitude on this point it is the fact that community studies and interpretations at historic sites do not remain long unchallenged.

If, then, the interpreter of history is never fully detached from his culture and he is a pointer of opinions and values, he must be careful not to twist his information. He should avoid the two extremes of becoming iconoclastic or uncritically reverential in his attitude toward his subject. As Michael Kammen points out in his Pulitzer Prize study *People of Paradox*, "American institutions have had too many uncritical lovers and too many unloving critics." What a responsible interpreter should not do is appeal to the passions of his visitors by uncritically enshrining or digging up dirt on historical personages. In keeping with the concept of guardianship, his responsibility is to examine critically past testimonies and facts, build interpretations from credible resources, and interpret what actually happened.

The interpreter of history in a local community, historic site, or museum also encounters another problem. He is never sure what facts to bring into his narrative. Though his craft is all-inclusive and covers everything from pots and pans to abstract ideas, a culture leaves him but a few vestiges of the doings of a few people. Given the fact that at best his narrative will represent but a thin slice of life, he is well-advised to consider in his interpretation the temper of earlier times, the sense of 'elan' in a culture. It is essential that he understand people and happenings in their contemporary setting and not in his. Otherwise, he may misjudge and misrepresent personalities and events.

Indeed, students of community history should become aware of a very important underpinning in historical interpretation, namely, that in history there are no simple explanations to events and issues. Consequently, the interpreter of historical events and personages should consider the many factors that have gone into the shaping of a culture. He should critically examine the contours and forces at work in society, thus the need for a close kinship among disciplines. Admittedly the historian can never reconstruct the total past; but he can restore part of a culture and share with his visitors a close approximation to the truth.

For example, the surviving artifacts—what we may properly call historical residues—tell us a great deal about people. The cook stove tells us much about the woman on the American frontier. In no uncertain terms, a study of material objects increases our understanding of American thought and culture. As Dr. Fred Schroeder tells us in "Seven Ways of Looking at an Artifact," published by the American Association for State and Local History in the November, 1976, issue of *History News*, there are different and complementary ways of reading an object. One can read with his hands—you get to feel the material, its construction. Doubtlessly, one can read an artifact with his eyes. In looking at a house, one may look at its corners, the doorways, the windows, the rooflines, or the cornices. One may study its design motifs. One can speculate on the function of an object, how it was used in its past surrounding. Also, one can explain features of an object in association with its environment. And, of course, cross-cultural comparisons of aspects of our material culture are extremely helpful in increasing our understanding of local and regional differences. It is important to remember, as the interpreter of history looks at the broad American setting, that Americans have spoken not only in different dialects, but they have also thought, built, and lived differently. Our surviving artifacts are the results of human events. They are the materials out of which history is told.

To be sure, many of man's material objects have intrinsic value. For example, buildings which demonstrate certain visual and architectural qualities, and objects which have particular design motifs, may possess asthetic appeal. But as far as the humanities are concerned the deeper value of an interpretation at an historic site or in a community lies in understanding how people coexisted with their buildings, physical objects, environments, and themselves.

In addition, houses, landscape, and physical objects demonstrate peoples' different tastes, skills, and interests. Any student of community history knows that house forms and landscape in America vary in distinctiveness from one section of the country to another. Differences in house structure and design, such as the Spanish Colonial house in the Southwest and the New England Colonial, give us insights into the skills of artisans, peoples' tastes, and their ability to adapt to local conditions. When properly studied these artifacts tell us a great deal about the residents. In his entertaining and imaginative study on *Civilization*, Kenneth Clark aptly noted that "If I had to say which was telling the truth about society, a speech by a minister of housing or the actual building put up in his time, I should believe the building."

In closing, I would like to mention that what helps sustain and inspire commitment to community ideas and values is their embodiment in an objective form that can be seen or touched. There are distinct values to ceremonial objects and places, historical societies, museums, and historic houses and districts. They afford people the opportunity to express as well as to reinforce attitudes, passions, values, and sentiments. A good scholarly example of the literary and cultural value of symbolism is Alan Trachtenberg's book on *Brooklyn Bridge*. First, he establishes the importance of Brooklyn Bridge as a cultural symbol. Second, he examines the process whereby the bridge, an artifact, became a symbol. Significantly, when individuals study a community and are able to draw varied meanings attached to peoples' activities and material artifacts and recall in their own words and expressions their perceptions about life in the community, they increase their understanding and appreciation of the diversities of human experience.

Using County Records in Writing Your Community's History

John J. Newman

The various speakers on local history for these seven workshops emphasized a variety of themes highlighting their attitude in approaching the study of local history. Fundamental to each, or any, approach to such study is research into the public records of the community. The degree of success of such research is dependent upon how systematic one is. Valid interpretations and conclusions flow from an understanding of the public sector of the community and its bureaucratic proclivity to perpetuate itself through records. Such record-creating practices assume greater value in offering continuity of data amassed over extended periods of time on most phases of the lives of its citizens. The success or failure of researching and writing the history of the community is dependent upon understanding the governmental structure of the community, especially on the local levels.

In approaching community history, or attempting to study any facet of it, one must first analyze the nature of the community itself, be it a town, township, or county. Consider the community in its life cycle and each element a phase of such life cycle. Ask questions: what is the legal base for this community? where would one find information concerning the platting of the community? its incorporation? its annexation? its dissolution? what records would one turn to in determining its economic base? its social base, including its social mores? its educational base, including such elements as fiscal creation, the training and education of students, on a township, county, and even a state level? Explore the cultural aspect of the community. For example, what is the history of public libraries in your community or county? Public records offer much information regarding transportation, including roads, toll roads, canals, and railroads. There are many other topics one could enumerate, as the nature of the people themselves: ethnic groups, minority groups (e.g., blacks), origin of the people who settled there through examination of naturalization records, or activities within the community through examination of military activities. Thus, the community can be viewed as an organic entity or as a specific microcosm for any one of a number of subjects.

In each of these examples, local public records permit one an opportunity for detailed examination. One cannot write community history without using government records.

What, then, is the nature of county government? In Indiana, local government units consist of the county itself, cities, towns, townships, school corporations, and public libraries. It is of paramount importance to note that each of these was created on a legal base, to serve official needs and not for any historical or genealogical purpose. The official actions, policies, and activities of government are documented in its records. The best level to research in any of these governmental subdivisions, I feel, is in county government records. Specific offices include the county recorder, the clerk of the circuit court, the auditor, the treasurer, and the county commissioners.

If one looks at the primary responsibilities of each of these officials, one quickly gains clues to what type of research should be performed in each office. For example, the county recorder does exactly that—he records. Primarily, he records land transfer records, economic encumbrances and mortgages against those land records, and miscellaneous records ranging from annual reports of toll road trustees to military discharge records. Over eighty different types of records are kept in his office. With the exception of deeds and mortgages, few are used by anyone for research.

The clerk of the circuit court has a dual function. Primarily his office serves as the official depository of the records of the judicial system in the county. These include a number of courts, such as a circuit court, possibly a superior court, a court of common pleas, a probate court, and a court of conciliation. Actions dealing with transfer of property through estates and guardianships, through handling civil causes, through criminal causes, as well as a variety of other functions, such as naturalizations, are filed in the clerk's office. Secondly, the clerk has specific responsibilities over and above his judicial ones. These include issuing certain types of licenses. One naturally goes to the clerk's office for marriage records, but he also licenses guns, poultry dealers and petty money lenders, and, until recently, physicians.

The auditor serves as the fiscal officer of the county in matters dealing with establishment of a tax base and determining the rate of taxes to be collected. Once money is received, he authorizes payment of this money to the county treasurer and keeps all bookkeeping records relating to such actions. The auditor also serves as secretary to several important offices. Most important of these are the county commissioners, the administrative, rule-making, policy-making body of the county, and when dealing with fiscal policy, in tandem with the county council.

Finally, the county treasurer serves as paymaster of the county. He collects funds through taxes, enters such into tax duplicates, and sees that money is paid.

Now, with these offices enumerated, let us review our community and examine some specific county records for information in writing a community history.

A community must have a legal base. Where would this be found? Usually individuals recorded the plat of the town in the plat books of the county recorder's office. As communities became more complex, they usually incorporated. One needs to go to the county commissioners' records to find a petition of incorporation and authorization for an election to be held and then the final order by the county commissioners for incorporating the community. The economic base of the community is reflected in the tax records, both in the assessed evaluation of the community—how much money was required for its operation—and in assessment of its private financial wealth in the appraisal process for determining taxation.

Indiana, through the years, has wrestled with various social questions. Among the most significant of these, for example, is the question of temperance. In the 1840s there was a swelling of interest in temperance throughout Indiana and by 1859 temperance leaders were able to control the retail liquor business in Indiana by having a law passed requiring sellers of intoxicating liquors to pay an annual $50 license fee and a $500 bond "conditioned that he will keep an orderly and peaceful house, and that he will pay all fines and costs that may be assessed against him, for any violations of the provisions of this act." When this law became effective, the town board of Brookville met by call, and "On motion of Jacob Bly the following resolution was offered to wit: Resolved, that in the opinion of the Board and Trustees of the Town of Brookville the Liquor Law passed at the last session of the Indiana Legislature is *unconstitutional* and that we cannot, in view of our oaths to support the Constitution of the State of Indiana, levy and tax or require any license to retail intoxicating liquors in the Corporation of the said Town of Brookville under the provisions of said Law." The resolution was adopted by a unanimous vote. (I might note that less than a year later, this law was ruled unconstitutional.)

However, government did continue to regulate liquor operations in the county by requiring anyone who sold intoxicating beverages to obtain a license by petition to the county commissioners. Such information was recorded at an early date in the county commissioners' record books and later in a separate liquor license book. When Prohibition came some individuals were permitted to make intoxicating liquor for medicinal, scientific, or religious purposes. These actions were regulated by the clerk of the circuit court. When Prohibition was repealed, the state created a statewide Alcoholic Beverage Commission, and local policy responsibilities regarding licensing of liquor were eliminated, except creation of a local board.

The 1816 Constitution set up a procedure whereby a percentage of the sale of lands in the county seat was to be used for establishing a county library. These public libraries existed until 1851 when they were replaced with township libraries attached to schools. Depending on the cultural growth of the county, separate public libraries began as early as the

1870s and continued with great impetus through the Carnegie Library building program after the turn of the century. The actions of the early county libraries, township public libraries, petitions, and other documentation to county officials, as well as records of their budgets through the years, are found in the auditor's office through county commissioners' records.

One area having significant social, economic, and political overtones is the question of transportation within the county. The enabling act creating Indiana and permitting it to form a Constitution stated that 2% of the sale of public lands was to be used for the creation of public or state roads throughout Indiana. It was, however, up to the local community to determine the location of these state roads. This responsibility fell to the county commissioners whose normal procedure was to receive a petition for a road, set up a road viewing committee, authorize a survey to be done, and to have all of these reports filed and recorded in the county commissioners' record before construction of the road. These roads developed helter-skelter, reflecting early concentrations of population within the county.

As the county became more industrialized and needed to move its produce to major markets, better road systems were required. After the 1850s the county frequently became a partner in the development of toll roads throughout the county. The constitution or bylaws were approved by the commissioners, usually the county purchased a certain amount of stock, and after 1878, because of their public trust, the toll road owners were to file an annual report, including assets, with the county recorder, usually found in the Miscellaneous Record.

In addition, the county was involved in the promotion of canals and had a long history in the development of railroads. They used the same approach with railroads as they did with toll roads; that is, they purchased stock, permitted surveys to be made, had railroad elections to determine whether the people within a township or area affected by the railroad would be willing to authorize the sale of bonds for the development of the railroad through the community. By the 1890s railroad corporations were required to file an annual report of their assets within the county with the county auditor's office. Again, this was used for taxing purposes, but one can get a list of the number of miles of track, including first rate track, secondary track, and what type of rolling stock was permanently located within the county.

Another important area where one can use local public records for assistance is population origin and mobility. Original land purchase ledgers many times show the settler's origin before he purchased land in the county. Records on citizens of foreign birth are found in naturalization records in the clerk's office and also in such records as the civil order record books where final authorization for citizenship occurred. Many of these petitions reflect not only vital statistical data about the individual but show his migrational pattern from the old world, not only to the new world, but within the new world before settling in the county where naturalized.

Minority groups are also recorded in public records. Very early records in southern Indiana reflect the fact that whites brought black slaves with them. Since slavery was outlawed under the Northwest Ordinance, these people entered into a contractual arrangement, probably illegal, with their slaves, indenturing them for a certain period of time, guaranteeing them certain rights, and then releasing them at the end of that period. These contracts are filed in the deed records because no other types of records were kept by the recorder at that time. These records usually end about 1820. The 1851 Constitution of Indiana prohibited the migration of blacks into the state. It required a Negro Register of all existing blacks. This record was kept by the clerk of the circuit court, and in many counties it is still available.

How should one proceed then? I would suggest that, no matter what your specific research topic is, you determine all you can about a subject using logic. For example, I will develop the theme of education. Ask yourself basic questions.

—When was it created?
—How was it funded?
—What is its organizational structure?
—What has been the role of government in this particular
  process?

Educational records seem to interest a great variety of
people but nothing definitive that I am aware of has been
done on this particular subject. To write a proper history of
education within the community, one must first establish
the fiscal base for the creation of the system. The Land
Ordinance of 1785 and the Northwest Ordinance set up the
concept for development of a financial base for supporting
public education. Section 16 of every congressional township was reserved for school purposes and served as this
economic base. This land was to be leased or sold with the
money being dedicated as a permanent fund for exclusive
use of education within that congressional township. Very
early, as a result of an 1818 law, the General Assembly
authorized the inhabitants of each congressional township
to incorporate for school purposes and to elect a congressional township clerk to determine the best procedures for
development of an educational system within that congressional township. These officials surveyed the land, many
times broke it up into smaller units as 20, 40, 60, or 120
acres, and then sold or leased these to the best bidder. One
would find in both the county commissioners' records and
in the recorder's office a base for these surveys and plats.

Once money was put into this dedicated account, it could
be loaned out, usually at 6% to 12% interest. The money
then was used exclusively for educational purposes. The interest, of course, was used for hiring teachers, building
schools, and similar activities. One will find school fund
mortgage record books in both the auditor's and the county
recorder's offices. These are valuable because the person
had to use his own land as security for the school fund loan;
usually there is a one line abstract for each sale, beginning
from federal government ownership to the time of the loan,
which gives one much economic data about that piece of

land. These records, as I said, had a very official value and of course weren't designed for research purposes. In Daviess County, the county auditor alledgedly set fire to the courthouse in 1894 to try to destroy these records because he was suspected of embezzling funds from the school mortgage account.

Once an incorporated township system was established, records reflect the actual educational process. The first level of development, as required under our 1816 Constitution, was the establishment of township schools. Prior to 1851 one or two township schools usually existed in each congressional township; school was conducted for several months or, perhaps, as many as six months. After the 1851 Constitution, the state took a stronger development towards education by authorizing a county superintendent who was to work with township trustees to improve education and was designated to systematize the record keeping and the educational processes. These records, if they currently exist, are either stored in an attic or basement of the courthouse since there no longer is a county superintendent, or they have been given to the superintendent of the school corporation which has replaced the old township school system.

In the recorder's records leases and deeds of gifts for half to an acre of land were given to these township trustees for school purposes. If one wants to determine the number of schoolhouses that have existed, deed record books would be a prime source to research. By the 1880s there was approximately one township school for every four square miles, and the old tradition of a person walking four or five miles to school is bunk in Indiana. But by the 1880s there was a trend towards higher education and the reorganization of the school system. Schools were located in the four outer regions of the congressional township, and a township high school was located in the center. By the turn of the century, horse and buggy "bussing" was occurring. Of course, this trend towards consolidation has continued into the present.

All records of these types of activities can be found in the auditor's office, including school enumerations, annual reports of the financial status of each school corporation filed with the county commissioners, and various petitions and other documentation concerning the development of schools. One also can turn to the circuit court records for lawsuits questioning the location of schools and use of funds.

Counties also were to have a county seminary. This was a secondary school, countywide, under the 1816 Constitution. Approximately sixty-five of the ninety-two counties in Indiana had county seminaries. Their sources of income were fines from breach of the penal code. Seminary trustees were appointed to receive these funds. When $600 was received, the trustees were authorized to construct a building. Annual reports of these trustees, as well as contracts for these buildings, frequently appear in the county commissioners' records. Because there was insufficient funding for county seminaries, they were eliminated by the 1851 Constitution, and those funds were turned over to the congressional school account. One final area of educational interest under early Indiana law is the county commissioners' ability to send two students from the county each year to one of the state universities. One will find as early as the 1830s through the turn of the century requests by individual students to be considered for this scholarship. Again, one can determine who went to school and perhaps even the policies used by county commissioners in determining eligibility for such a scholarship.

By using education as a specific example of how to proceed, I hope I have given you a feeling that there is a wealth of information existing within these records. Much of what I have given to you today I realize you cannot grasp so rapidly. Thus, I would like to suggest certain guides you can use to determine what functions government performs and what functions caused records to be created that would be of specific benefit in your research. The prime source of information about county government is the published WPA Historic Records Surveys. The description of records existing within each office currently is obsolete. However, the history of the laws and the subject citations of all functions performed by these county governmental units is of pertinent value today. I would suggest that you use the Warrick County WPA inventory which is valuable for its history of territorial laws and the Tippecanoe County WPA inventory for its overall concept of county government. These two WPA inventories, found in many public libraries throughout Indiana, can be of great help in determining what record books might contain information on the subject you are researching.

There might be a second approach to research about your community, and I will briefly mention this. You may only be concerned in making community data available to others. For example, you may want to develop a list of the incorporated communities within your county; a list of schools; a list of county, city, town, township public officials; or even an inventory of the records within government offices. As I have illustrated before, answers to these questions are contained within the public records themselves; for example, it is a matter of using election records in the clerk's office, or various other specific records, to determine what sources would be available.

Whatever your approach, collect data in a systematized structure. What do we keep? What do we as local historical societies collect? With whom do we compete and who are the competitors? We can't keep everything; the volume is too great. (Our current governor, Otis R. Bowen, has an estimated two to two and one half million items in his official papers. That volume overwhelms us!) As government becomes more complex two growths of records develop: (1) the sheer volume of the number of records, cases, or units of records, and (2) the complexity of the documentation within each file itself.

Thus, as members of local historical societies, we must both define our purpose, our mission, and determine what areas of community record keeping fit into our mission statement; then we must collect only those records which fit into that structure. Do it systematically. Define the nature and structure of the record creating agency. See what records it created. Determine which of those records have research value—not only to the genealogist or local historian but to the academic historian as well. Learn who else is collecting what. Co-operate, share, exchange—all within a predetermined, defined system.

I have been state archivist for ten years and during this period have noticed little use, *in an organized manner,* of government records in development of local history in Indiana. There are certain trends developing, including demographic history, in which one is interested in the totality of a segment of society and its effect internally and externally. Various graduate history students have used local records to great advantage. But written local history, as evidenced recently during the Bicentennial, has generated very little original research into existing government records. I note mistakes of earlier histories perpetuated in the newer volumes. Research into county records and local political subdivision records, in connection with other types of records, can serve as an excellent means for the development of accurate, comprehensive local history within your community.

COUNTY AUDITOR (1841–current)

(Duties previously performed by Clerk of the Circuit Court)
Records usually in Auditor's office

Type of record	Dates	Comments
1) Register of Orders (warrants) issued	1841–1924	Lists every check authorized for payment by auditor, its number, date, to whom paid, and reason. Gives complete comprehensive cost of county government; also valuable for social and economic history.
2) Transfer Books	c. 1841–current	Done every 4 years; shows record of transfer of ownership of real estate in county. Arranged by taxing units.
3) Assessment Record	c. 1841–(dates vary)	From beginning of county to 1841 known as assessment rolls; unbound and dates vary for real and personal property, 1841–1891; 1891 usually bound by taxing unit (personal property). Good for enumeration of personal property to 1950s. Usually destroyed in most counties because of bulk.
4) Assessor's Plat Book (map)	c. 1841–current	Done every 4 years in reference to transfer books; shows plat of each taxing unit and land and owners' names. Many for 19th century destroyed.
5) Township Trustees' Annual Reports	1859–current	Shows expenditures of township by fund (roads, schools, etc.), sometimes narrative account of expenditures. Few found for 19th century.
6) Register of School Fund Loans	c. 1865–current	Shows date, type and amount of loan, mortgager, and description of property.
7) Enumeration of White and Colored Males over 21 years	1820–1955	1820–1850 every 5 years; 1850–1955 every 7 years; shows name of male, age (after 1860s), arranged by township. Rare before 1870s.

COUNTY COMMISSIONERS c. 1817–present
(Records in Auditor's office, or in storage)

Type of record	Dates	Comments
1) County Commissioners' Record	beginning of county-current	Records administrative actions of the county; all functions of county go through this office; usually indexed by volume; for few counties separate accumulative index.
2) Claim and Allowance Docket	1860s–current	Records each payment authorized by commissioners; date, amount, to whom, reason. Good for building improvements, roads, etc.
3) Burial record of soldiers, sailors, marines	1889–c. 1901	Shows cost of burial, location, service, and personal data on veteran.
4) Liquor retailers bond record	c. 1867–1918	Bond of retailer, location, and brief description of place of business; prior bonds in commissioners record.
5) Blue prints	varies	Of public buildings, bridges (esp. covered), roads; retention varies from county to county.
6) Road record	c. beginning of county (varies) to current	Record of road contracts, date, location, and description (see also Commissioners' Record).
7) Ditch record	c. 1872–current	Data varies from petitions, surveys, bond issues, construction, and maintenance.

COUNTY RECORDER 1790 +
(Most records in office)

Note: Official began with one book—deeds: c. 1848 separate mortgage record; 1850s–1870 separate miscellaneous record; 1870s–1900s separate Chattel Mortgage Record; today over seventy separate types of records.

Type of record	Dates	Comments
1) Deed record	Beginning of county–current	Records transfer of title to real property (see note).
2) Cemetery deed records	1925–current	Records deeds to cemetery plots (see note).
3) Tract book	beginning of county	Records by legal description sale of land from U.S. government to individual. Shows section of land, township, range-name, actual residence, and date.
4) Plat book	dates vary–current	Shows plats of subdivisions: towns, cemeteries, etc. (see note).
5) Mortgage record	c. 1848–current	Shows mortgage for property (see note); good for social and economic history.
6) Chattel Mortgage Record	1870s–1900s–1935	Mortgages of personal property (see note); good for social and economic history.
7) Miscellaneous Record	1850s–1870s–current	Records a variety of records, both required by law and at individual's discretion, as turnpike reports, leases, election returns for churches, organizations, Bible pages, etc.; usually indexed by name only for each volume. Browse!
8) Record of Indentures	c. 1830–c. 1910 varies	Record of children indentured to citizens to learn trade (usually orphaned children).
9) [Soldiers] Discharge Record	1865–current	Record of discharge of soldiers, sailors, and marines in Civil War and later wars.
10) Register of farm names	1913–current	Record of farm names registered by owners (infrequently recorded).

COUNTY RECORDER *(Cont.)*

Type of record	Dates	Comments
11) Record of Marks and Brands	19th century (varies)	Record of animal brands and marks by owners—good if person never owned land but recorded the brands.
12) Newspapers	c. 1852–current	Permissive legislation; recorder, if ordered by commissioners, will keep file of papers of two political parties, about 45 counties did so; few counties (under 25) have files currently.

COUNTY TREASURER 1817–present
(Most noncurrent records are in storage)

Type of record	Dates	Comments
1) Tax Duplicates	1841–present	Record of taxes payable, name of taxpayer and taxing unit; value of real and personal property; amount of taxes and payment. Good for historical and genealogical purposes, for economic and social history, and genealogical data.

Nearly All Other Records Duplicated in Auditor's Office

CLERK OF THE CIRCUIT COURT 1790–current
Records in office or storage

NOTE: The clerk has three major responsibilities: 1) he is the records agent for the judiciary; 2) he files non-judicial records (e.g., licensing); and 3) he is chief election officer (1937+). The clerk performs three major functions: 1) he files original papers; 2) he records pleadings and papers into ledger books; and 3) he generates the official record of court proceedings, in order books and related ledgers. It is especially important to note that research data may be in only one functional record. Thus pleadings in a judicial action are rarely recorded in an order book except by reference. The researcher must look at both records. Over 600 different types of records have been generated in this office. Use the Tippecanoe County WPA Historical Records Inventory as a guide.

COURTS—LOCAL LEVEL—INDIANA
TERRITORIAL COURTS

Type of record	Dates	Comments
1) General Quarter Sessions of the Peace		Criminal, Administrative ("County Business"); Knox 6/20/1790—12/31/1805; Clark 2/03/1801—12/31/1805; Dearborn 3/07/1801—12/31/1805.
2) Circuit Court (of General Court) Criminal		Justices of Assize, Justices of Oyer and Terminer, and Jail Delivery, Nisi Prius 1788—9/10/1814. Knox 6/20/1790—12/31/1813; 9/10/1814—General Court met at Vincennes and Brookville; Clark 2/3/1801—12/31/1813 (?); Dearborn 3/7/1803—12/31/1813; 12/31/1813—9/10/1814 General Court refused to ride circuit.
3) Court of Common Pleas		Civil; Knox 6/20/1790—12/31/1805; Clark 2/3/1801—12/31/1805; Dearborn 3/7/1803—12/31/1805.
4) Probate Court		Probate; Knox 6/20/1790—12/31/1805; Clark 2/3/1801—12/31/1805; Dearborn 3/7/1803—12/31/1805.
5) Orphans' Court	10/1/1795—12/31/1805	Knox 10/1/1795—12/31/1805; Clark 2/3/1801—12/31/1805; Dearborn 3/7/1803—12/31/1805.
6) Court of Common Pleas	10/1/1805—12/31/1813	Civil, Criminal, Probate, Administrative ("County Business"); Knox 1/1/1806—12/31/1813; Clark 1/1/1806—12/31/1813; Dearborn 1/1/1806—12/1/1813; Harrison 12/1/1808—12/31/1813; Jefferson 1/1/1811—12/31/1813; Franklin 1/1/1811—12/31/1813; Wayne 1/1/1811—12/31/1813; Warrick 4/1/1813—12/31/1813.

COURTS—LOCAL LEVEL—INDIANA
TERRITORIAL COURTS (Cont.)

Type of record	Dates	Comments
Legally no local courts	12/31/1813–8/30/1814	Washington 1/17/1814; Judges of General Court, appointed federally, refused to ride circuit.
6a) Circuit Court		
7) Circuit Court	8/30/1814–	Civil, Criminal, Probate, Administrative ("County Business"); Chancery 9/10/1814; Switzerland 10/1/1814; Perry 11/1/1814; Posey 11/1/1814; Jackson 1/1/1816; Orange 2/1/1816.

COURTS—LOCAL LEVEL—INDIANA
Under First Constitution 1816–1851

Type of record	Dates	Comments
1) Circuit Court	1817–1853	For all territorial counties and for all counties as created. Consisted of one judge who rode circuit and two locally elected associate judges.
2) Probate Court	1829–1853	Note: From 1825–1829 associate judges constituted a probate court as part of the circuit court. For all counties in existence during this period.
3) Court of Common Pleas	1849–1953	Marion County; Tippecanoe County

Under Current Constitution

Type of record	Dates	Comments
1) Circuit Court	1851–current	For all counties (Newton 1859–)
2) Court of Common Pleas	1852–1873	For all counties (Newton 1859–)
3) Court of Conciliation	1852–1865	For all counties (Newton 1859–1865)

4) County Court c. 1975–current (Replaces Justices of the Peace); handles misdemeanor causes and civil pleadings under $1,500. Dates and titles vary according to county.

5) Superior Court dates vary For some counties replaced court of common pleas. Courts still being established. Use WPA Inventory as guide for county you are researching.
Note: These courts were not "superior" or above the circuit court, only an additional court. One needs to search these judicial records as well as the circuit court records in the county.

6) Other courts

COURT SUBJECT MATTER ORIGINAL JURISDICTION

Type of record	Dates	Comments
1) Civil Actions at Law	1813 1814+ 1838–1853 1853–1872	(a) Circuit Court 1 judge of General Court (b) Circuit Court (c) Probate Court (d) Court of Common Pleas (e) Superior Court
2) Criminal Cases	1813 1814+ 1806–, 1813; 1853–1872	(a) Circuit Court 1 Judge of General Court (b) Circuit Court (c) Court of Common Pleas
3) Chancery Cases	1813 1814+ 1838–1853 1813; 1853–1872	(a) Circuit Court 1 Judge of General Court (b) Circuit Court (c) Probate Court (d) Court of Common Pleas (e) Superior Court

COURT SUBJECT MATTER (Cont.)

Type of record	Dates	Comments
4) Probate Matters, Settlement of Decedants' estates and guardianships	1790–1805 1795–1805 1814–1829; 1873+ 1829–1853 1813; 1853–1873	(a) Probate Court (b) Orphans' Court (c) Circuit Court (d) Probate Court (e) Court of Common Pleas
5) Juvenile Matters	1867+ 1867–1873	(a) Circuit Court (b) Court of Common Pleas
6) Conciliation	1853–1865	(a) Court of Conciliation
7) Naturalization Proceedings	1814+ 1813, 1853–1873	(a) Circuit Court (b) Court of Common Pleas (c) Superior Court

MARRIAGE RECORDS
(Shows complexity of just one type of record)

Type of record	Dates	Comments
1) Record Books	Beginning of county to post-1905	A. License/return books
	1905–early 1920s possibly	B. Application Books
	1905–present	C. Application/license/return books
	2/1882–2/1905	D. "Record of Return of Marriage"
	1905–1949	E. Board of Health Application Books
	dates vary	F. Indices (Volume, General, WPA, Private, Card, etc.)

2) Original Papers

G. Affidavit Books (rare) — dates vary, usually from the 1870s to about 1905

A. Licenses/returns — c. 1870s
   Preprinted forms, usually have affidavits of age, residence with file
   Printed forms — c. 1870s–present
B. Affidavit of age
C. Affidavit of residence
D. Original Applications — 2/1905–
   (a) male (Form #33) — 2/1905–
   (b) female (Form #35)
Note: These sheets served as worksheets for 1(B) above and were used from 2/1905 until about 1920 or later depending on the county. As alternative entries were made directly into the Application/License/Return books 1(C).
E. Blood tests. These are confidential. — 3/1/1940–present
F. Clerk's Monthly Report to State Board of Health — usually 1959+
G. Record of Marriage Form to State Board of Health, dates vary.
H. County Board of Health Report — 1907–1943
I. Certified Copy of Marriage Record — dates vary

NOTE: There are dozens of other valuable records for research. The person who does not consult the WPA Inventories referred to in the article is shortchanging himself. Read both the introductory section for each office—to learn functions and procedures and examine the types of records listed.

Indiana's Historical Services, and Beyond

Pamela J. Bennett

Resources for local historical societies in Indiana are plentiful. Both private organizations and governmental agencies offer a multitude of services and information and make available a moderate level of funding such that an historical society should be able to progress in various programs ranging from archives and oral history to historic preservation. The major problem for most groups—aside from achieving a desired level of funding—is knowing what agencies exist and what functions they perform. Since there are both private and governmental responsibilities functioning concurrently in most fields, the problem is compounded. The diversity may be confusing at the outset, but once oriented an historical organization can find help for its problems. The accompanying chart illustrates the diversity; the narrative following provides some orientation. It rests with the historical society to seek out the answers for its particular needs.[1]

There are two statewide organizations available for general historical aid, the Indiana Historical Society and the Indiana Historical Bureau.[2] The **Indiana Historical Society** is a private nonprofit membership organization founded in 1830 and chartered by the Indiana General Assembly. Individual membership benefits include volumes of the *Publications* and other books (free or at a discount), the quarterly *Indiana Magazine of History* published by the Indiana University History Department, the monthly *Indiana History Bulletin* published by the Indiana Historical Bureau, a newsletter, and section publications in family history and genealogy, military and medical history, and archaeology. The Society is well endowed and in a position to enrich the Indiana historical community with various historical and cultural programs and activities. The Society works with local historical groups primarily through the developmental work of Thomas Krasean. The Society maintains a separate research library in the State Library and Historical Building; the Society library also is sponsoring field work, workshops, and programs to improve the collection of Indiana materials. The Society is project oriented with present programs in newspaper history, preparing an Indiana guide similar to the WPA guide, microfilming of newspapers, and tape recording state and local history for the blind and physically handicapped. The Society also co-sponsors the Indiana Junior Historical Society with the Indiana Historical Bureau.

Contact: Gayle Thornbrough, Executive Secretary, Indiana Historical Society, 315 West Ohio Street, Indianapolis, Indiana 46202; (317) 232-1882.

The **Indiana Historical Bureau** is a state agency established and governed by Indiana Code 4-23-7, the Indiana Library and Historical Department Act. The Bureau was established in 1915 as the Indiana Historical Commission, and since that time it has established a strong publication program with the *Indiana Historical Collections* which are distributed free to Indiana public libraries and sold to the general public. In addition to publishing Indiana history materials, the Bureau's general statutory charge includes encouraging the teaching of history in the schools and working with local historical societies. The Bureau manages the printshop in the State Library and Historical Building and is therefore able to produce materials distributed free to teachers of Indiana history; the shop also produces publications and materials for the Indiana Historical Society and the Indiana State Library. The Bureau publishes the monthly *Indiana History Bulletin* which contains historical articles, book reviews, and publication and activity news from, and of interest to, local historical societies. The Bureau is involved in a broad range of activities such as the state Governors' Portraits Collection, the Centennial History of the Indiana General Assembly, the Indiana American Revolution Bicentennial Commission, the

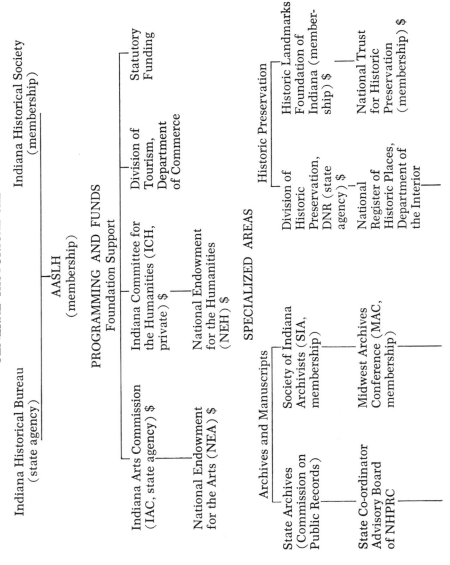

GENERAL HISTORICAL AID

Indiana Historical Society
(membership)

Indiana Historical Bureau
(state agency)

AASLH
(membership)

PROGRAMMING AND FUNDS
Foundation Support

Indiana Arts Commission
(IAC, state agency) $

National Endowment
for the Arts (NEA) $

Indiana Committee for
the Humanities (ICH,
private) $

National Endowment
for the Humanities
(NEH) $

Division of
Tourism,
Department
of Commerce

Statutory
Funding

SPECIALIZED AREAS

Archives and Manuscripts

State Archives
(Commission on
Public Records)

State Co-ordinator
Advisory Board
of NHPRC

Society of Indiana
Archivists (SIA,
membership)

Midwest Archives
Conference (MAC,
membership)

Historic Preservation

Division of
Historic
Preservation,
DNR (state
agency) $

National
Register of
Historic Places,
Department of
the Interior

Historic Landmarks
Foundation of
Indiana (member-
ship) $

National Trust
for Historic
Preservation
(membership) $

NHPRC $

Society of American Archivists (SAA, membership)

HUD Historic Preservation Loans $

Oral History

Libraries

Public Library
ALSA
Indiana State Library
Indiana Library and Historical Board, LSCA $
┌ InCOLSA (membership)
├ Indiana Library Association-Indiana Library Trustees
├ Indiana Library Association (ILA-ILTA, membership)
└ American Library Association (ALA, membership)

Museums

Section of Museums, DHP, DNR
Institute of Museum Services $
Smithsonian Institution, National Museum Act $
NEA
NEH
┌ Association of Indiana Museums (AIM, membership)
├ Midwest Museums Conference
└ American Association of Museums (AAM, membership)

Oral History

Oral History Project, Indiana State Library
Oral History Research Project, Indiana University
┌ Oral History Roundtable (membership)
└ National Oral History Association (membership)

STATE LEGISLATION FOR FUNDING

Indiana Code

Historical Society General 17-3-86	Historical Society Museums 19-7-47

Commission on Public Records, George Rogers Clark Day, and historical markers.

Co-sponsorship of the **Indiana Junior Historical Society** (IJHS)[3] is an important part of the educational program of the Bureau. The IJHS is a federation of history clubs throughout the state and involves young people from elementary through high school in historical programs and activities. The IJHS also sponsors workshops for teachers of Indiana history. The director is Robert Kirby; the assistant director is Debra Fausset.

Contact: Pamela J. Bennett, Director, Indiana Historical Bureau, 140 North Senate Avenue, Room 408, Indianapolis, Indiana 46204; (317) 232-2537.

No historical organization interested in developing program areas can afford to be without the benefits of the **American Association for State and Local History** (AASLH), a non-profit educational organization dedicated to advancing knowledge and appreciation of local history in the United States and Canada. Membership includes the monthly *History News* with its valuable technical leaflets, educational programs including both workshops and slide-tape presentations, job placement, a consultation service, and discounts on AASLH publications. The AASLH provides expert help and materials for all aspects of local history operations. A best buy!

Contact: AASLH, 1400 Eighth Avenue South, Nashville, Tennessee 37203.

PROGRAMMING AND FUNDS

Funding was indicated as the major problem for many historical societies, and the organization chart indicates agencies having regular grant programs with a dollar sign ($). Area related programs are discussed in separate sections, but two state organizations and their federal counterparts provide funding in a variety of areas and also provide expert help in programming.

Most important for historical societies judging by recent performance is the **Indiana Committee for the Humanities** (ICH). The October, 1979, issue of AASLH's *History News* focused on the resources of state based humanities committees. A feature on the ICH by Mark Rozeen is included, and Rozeen's point is clear: local history has become a major interest of the ICH and local historical societies have benefited. Besides various types and sizes of grants, the ICH has a resource center (with a free catalog) of humanities projects materials available for use. A newsletter is free upon request as well. The ICH is an independent nonprofit group of Indiana citizens working in co-operation with the National Endowment for the Humanities, the source of most grant monies. Consultation on programs and possible grant requests is encouraged.

Contact: The Indiana Committee for the Humanities, 4200 Northwestern Avenue, Indianapolis, Indiana 46208; (317) 925-5316.

The **Indiana Arts Commission** (IAC) is a state agency governed by Indiana Code 4-23-2 and was created to encourage public participation and interest in the arts and cultural activities. The IAC uses both state funds and National Endowment for the Arts (NEA) funds to provide, on a matching grants basis, for a broad array of program areas. Two areas of special interest to historical groups are museums and folk arts. The IAC at present has a museums co-ordinator, Andrea Pactor, through an NEA grant; a state folk arts co-ordinator is also in future planning. The IAC has a free newsletter which provides funding deadlines and information about people and activities throughout the state. The IAC also has available materials for the National Endowment for the Arts. Consultation on programs and grant requests is encouraged.

Contact: Janet I. Harris, Executive Director, Indiana Arts Commission, 155 East Market Street, Suite 614, Indianapolis, Indiana 46204; (317) 232-1268.

The **National Endowment for the Arts** and the **National**

Endowment for the Humanities (NEH) both have many funding opportunities for historical societies. Program guides and deadlines are available each year from these agencies in Washington, D.C.

Historical societies should not neglect to explore funding opportunities from private foundations as well. The Foundation Center at the main Indianapolis-Marion County Public Library provides resources on foundations throughout Indiana and the United States; patrons must conduct their own searches. A 1976 *Guide to Indiana Foundations* by James H. Taylor was compiled from Internal Revenue Service records and lists 334 foundations, noting interest areas and giving sample grants. Local corporations often have foundations which are willing to contribute to appropriate projects. There are also state laws which provide funding for historical societies; those laws are discussed and the texts provided in a separate section of this article. (See below, pp. 91-98)

The **Division of Tourism,** Department of Commerce, has a program which many historical groups have used. Limited funds are available on a matching basis for brochures which publicize activities and sites which enhance Indiana's tourist potential. Concurrently the tourist potential of anything historical is being realized and exploited for the benefit generally of those historical things.

Contact: Division of Tourism, Department of Commerce, 336 State House, Indianapolis, Indiana 46204; (317) 232-8860.

SPECIALIZED AREAS
Archives and Manuscripts

Once again, help for historical societies with archives and manuscripts is available both in the public and the private sector. Funding from granting institutions is probably most difficult to obtain for projects in this area. The library of the Indiana Historical Society and divisions of the Indiana State Library are willing to give advice in certain manuscript areas. The **Indiana State Archives,** a division of the Commission on Public Records, is the depository for the records of the various departments and officers of state government. The head of the archives works throughout the state to advise local organizations and local governmental units on the proper care and maintenance of their collections and records. The conservation laboratory (shared with the Indiana Historical Society) can provide guidance and instruction on conservation and restoration and, as time permits, can contract for conservation work of a serious nature.

Contact: John J. Newman, State Archivist, 140 North Senate Avenue, Indianapolis, Indiana 46204; (317) 232-3737.

One established grant program exists in the area of archives and manuscripts through the **National Historical Publications and Records Commission** (NHPRC). The NHPRC is a federal program, which grew out of the National Historical Publications Commission according to 1974 legislation, Public Law 93-536, that is part of the National Archives and Records Service of the General Services Administration. The 1974 law effected the commission's name change and authorized it to begin assisting state and local organizations in the preservation, arrangement, and description of historical records. The commission publishes a free newsletter *Annotation,* which updates grant programs and guidelines. The original thrust of the commission continues with the subsidy of scholarly letterpress and microfilm editions of papers of selected historical figures.

Contact: NHPRC, National Archives and Records Service, Washington, D.C. 20408.

The 1974 NHPRC legislation mandated a mechanism to assure state input into the new records program. Federal guidelines call for a state co-ordinator (either the state archivist or the state historian) and an advisory board appointed by the governor; this state board must formulate a state records plan,[4] must review and make recommendations regarding grant proposals to NHPRC from organizations within the state, and may suggest or administer grants for records projects. All grants submitted to NHPRC must also be sent to the state co-ordinator, John J. Newman, for review by the state board; the national commission will not consider proposals without state input. Unfortunately, the program has had large problems on both the state and national levels since its inception; first and foremost has been the matter of budget. These problems and some speculations about the future have been the subject of sessions at recent major historical meetings and have been aired in writing by Larry J. Hackman, Director of the NHPRC records program.[5] Indiana has a poor record in the number of applications for grants as well as for grants funded under this program.

Help in archival areas is available also from nonprofit membership organizations on the state, regional, and national level. The **Society of Indiana Archivists** (SIA) strives to bring together archivists and manuscript holders and administrators with users of such holdings to promote the best preservation and use of historical research materials. Semiannual meetings with educational programs, an occasional newsletter, and publications are benefits of membership.

Contact: Thomas Krasean, SIA Secretary-Treasurer, Indiana Historical Society, 315 West Ohio Street, Indianapolis, Indiana 46202; (317) 232-1881.

The SIA promotes contact with other state archival groups and with the regional **Midwest Archives Conference** (MAC) and the national **Society of American Archivists** (SAA). MAC and SAA provide broader resources in publications and programs. They are especially aware that many, if not most, administrators of archival and manuscript collections are not trained archivists, and the SAA in particular has emphasized basic training and materials.

Contact: James E. Fogerty, MAC Secretary-Treasurer, Minnesota Historical Society, 1500 Mississippi Street, St. Paul, Minnesota 55101; SAA, 330 South Wells Street, Suite 810, Chicago, Illinois 60606.

Historic Preservation

Implementation of federal historic preservation programs was slow in Indiana, and, perhaps as a result, there has been a very strong program in the private sector. The National Historic Preservation Act of 1966 established a program of matching grants-in-aid for the acquisition and development of properties listed on the **National Register of Historic Places.** The federal program originates in the Department of the Interior, and the state program is situated in the Department of Natural Resources with its head, Joseph Cloud, as the State Historic Preservation Officer (SHPO). The SHPO, with the help of an advisory council and a staff specified in part by the federal legislation, determines nominations for the National Register and processes all applications for available federal funds. Although Indiana participated in the federal programs, it was not in full compliance with federal law until the General Assembly in 1977 established the **Division of Historic Preservation** within the Department of Natural Resources under Indiana Code 14-3-3.3. The division consists of four sections: 1) archaeology, 2) registration and survey, 3) museums, and 4) historic sites and structures. Overall the division is to provide information, advise and co-ordinate activities of local groups, provide technical and financial assistance to local groups, review environmental impact statements, develop a state survey of historical, architectural, and archaeological resources, and prepare a state preservation plan. Specifically, the section of registration and survey is in charge of the National Register program in Indiana and administers the federal preservation grants programs. Relatively new funding opportunities for historic preservation can also be explored through this division: tax incentives for rehabilitation of historic buildings under the Tax Reform Act of 1976 and the older (1974) Department of Housing and Urban Development (HUD) historic preservation loans. Historic preservation at the federal level is in the process of changing drastically; the present situation and future possibilities are discussed, for example, in the April, 1980, *History News.*

Contact: Division of Historic Preservation, DNR, Indiana State Museum, 202 North Alabama, Indianapolis, Indiana 46204; (317) 232-1637.

In the private sector historic preservation in Indiana achieved its initial impetus with the founding in 1960, under the auspices of Eli Lilly, of **Historic Landmarks Foundation of Indiana** (HLFI). Today HLFI is a well-endowed nonprofit membership organization which is dedicated to promoting restoration and preservation and to increasing public awareness of the benefits of historic preservation. Indianapolis contains the state office and a local office, and there are regional offices in South Bend and Cambridge City. Professional staffs administer historic properties, act as consultants, conduct surveys, and carry out public education programs such as workshops, lectures, tours, and the continuing Town Tour program in individual communities throughout the state. HLFI maintains a resource center of books and periodicals at its state office, which is open for all members to use. A quarterly newsletter, occasional publications, and bulletins on technical advice and legislation are rich resources for members. A recent (1977) addition to HLFI's list of services is a State-wide Revolving Loan Fund.

Contact: J. Reid Williamson, Jr., President, HLFI, 3402 Boulevard Place, Indianapolis, Indiana 46208; (317) 926-2301.

Another membership organization which offers help and resources for historic preservation is the **National Trust for Historic Preservation,** chartered by the United States Congress in 1949 to further a national policy of preservation and to facilitate public participation in the preservation movement. The Trust offers a multitude of programs in consultation and education, maintains historic properties, and conducts meetings, conferences, and workshops. The Trust has programs of grants and loans. Members receive a monthly newsletter and a quarterly journal.

Contact: National Trust, 1785 Massachusetts Avenue, N.W., Washington, D.C. 20036; Midwest Office, National Trust, 1800 South Prairie Avenue, Chicago, Illinois 60616.

Libraries

In fulfilling its mission to preserve local history an historical society cannot afford to ignore the resources available through a local public library and the Indiana library network. Many public libraries work with historical groups on collections and programs; some very successful co-operative relationships have resulted. The research network established by public libraries, Area Library Service Authorities (ALSAs), and the Indiana State Library can be essential to historical projects; the TWX system allows for rapid contact with the State Library for information or loan of certain items.[6]

Through its various divisions the **Indiana State Library** offers a wide range of information, resources, and practical help. The Indiana Division has manuscripts, books, and state government publications, manages the state document depository system, and has a field agent in oral history; it also has the most complete collection of Indiana newspapers in the state. The Genealogy Division has a magnificent collection of resources for local history and family research, including journals of state historical agencies throughout the United States and census records. The Reference and Loan Division has charge of all federal documents and administers computer based information systems. The Extension Division works with libraries throughout the state to provide help and information; it also administers the programs of certification and funding which go through the State Library.

Contact: C. Ray Ewick, Director, Indiana State Library, 140 North Senate Avenue, Indianapolis, Indiana 46204; (317) 232-3692.

The **Indiana Library and Historical Board** is the five member governing body of the department consisting of the State Library and the Historical Bureau. By state law all funds for libraries from the federal government under the Library Services and Construction Act (LSCA) are allotted by this board. Guidelines for funds have allowed for some historically important projects, but the limits are narrow. The directors of the State Library and the Historical Bureau are ex-officio members of the board; quarterly meetings are open to the public.

Two private membership organizations have a potential value for local historical groups: **Indiana Co-operative Library Services Authority** (InCOLSA) and the **Indiana Library As-**

sociation—**Indiana Library Trustees Association** (ILA-ILTA). InCOLSA was organized in 1974 and is supported by public funds and user fees. Among its goals is an on-line computer base of Indiana materials; this goal could involve historical organizations as users or as members because of holdings appropriate for the data base.

Contact: InCOLSA, 1100 West 42nd Street, Indianapolis, Indiana 46208; (317) 926-3361.

The ILA-ILTA (at the same address) has demonstrated an increased interest in working on local history oriented projects and with local history groups under its new director, Elbert Watson. The need to pool local resources for local interests and needs in cultural areas will become even more necessary as all sources of funds tighten; the natural ties between libraries as repositories and historical groups as collectors and preservers of local history should be cultivated or strengthened depending upon current situations.

Museums

Resources and funding for museums and museum programs are probably the most broadly based of any area discussed in this article. For example, museums have funding opportunities in no less than four separate federal programs: 1) Museum Programs of the National Endowment for the Arts, 2) the Museums and Historical Organizations Program, Division of Public Programs, of the National Endowment for the Humanities, 3) the National Museum Act, administered by the Smithsonian Institution, and 4) the Institute of Museum Services. General guidelines, available 1980 deadlines, administrators, and addresses for federal programs are given in the February, 1980, *History News*. It is imperative if an organization is to be successful in receiving grants, that it be on regular mailing lists for all of the relevant programs. State legislation for historical museum funding is discussed in a separate section of this article.

Resources for museums within the state of Indiana are also available in both the public and private sector. Along with the Indiana Arts Commission, the **Indiana State Museum** in the **Section of Museums** of the Division of Historic Preservation, Department of Natural Resources, is the arm of state government with specific responsibility in this area. According to Indiana *Acts* 1977, Public Law 163, the Section of Museums shall "assist other museums within the state to meet the criteria of museum accreditation." The State Museum houses the administrative offices of the Division of Historic Preservation and serves as the repository for the material remains of the state's history. A private nonprofit membership organization, the Indiana State Museum Society, assists in the programs of the State Museum.

Contact: Carl Armstrong, Director, Division of Historic Preservation, DNR, Indiana State Museum, 202 North Alabama, Indianapolis, Indiana 46204; (317) 232-1637.

As in several other areas, a nonprofit membership organization has been formed in the museums field to serve the needs and interests of local groups in the state. The **Association of Indiana Museums** (AIM) membership ranges from local historical groups to art museums to zoos. AIM provides two workshops each year plus a newsletter and occasional publications to keep members informed.

Contact: Margaret Sallee, AIM Treasurer, Benjamin Harrison Home, 1230 North Delaware, Indianapolis, Indiana 46202; (317) 631-1898.

At the national level museums can look to the **American Association of Museums** (AAM) for materials and services including museum accreditation. AAM has six regional conferences which share in the governing body of the organization; Indiana is in the Midwest Museums Conference and hosted the 1979 meeting of that group providing further educational opportunities for local museum personnel.

Oral History

The final resource area for discussion is relatively new as a specific field of interest even though oral history is obviously one of the oldest forms of transmitting history and tradition. Oral history projects are increasingly more popular among local groups, and there are several places to turn for help. The **Oral History Project** of the Indiana Division, Indiana State Library, is a concentrated effort to document Indiana history through the medium of oral history interviews. The field agent who directs the project also is available to advise groups and individuals who want to conduct oral history projects. A free brochure is available.

Contact: F. Gerald Handfield, Jr., Field Agent, Indiana Division, Indiana State Library, 140 North Senate Avenue, Indianapolis, Indiana 46204; (317) 232-3672.

There is also an **Oral History Research Project** located at Indiana University. Personnel have limited availability for local consultation. The Indiana Historical Society has also evidenced interest in this field through support of the Indiana University project.

The nonprofit membership organization, the Indiana **Oral History Roundtable** grew out of the State Library's Oral History Project and the increased interest in local history on the local level. Its main purpose is to provide a forum for discussion as well as guidance and assistance in oral history projects. The Roundtable has at least two workshop meetings per year and a quarterly newsletter. Membership is available through the Indiana Division, Indiana State Library.

Funding for oral history projects can be obtained from various organizations depending upon the thrust of the project. The humanities organizations have been especially open to such projects.

STATE LEGISLATION FOR FUNDING

At the present time two sections of the Indiana Code provide funding for historical societies by counties and units of local government. IC 17-3-86 dates from 1929 and is very general in its provisions; IC 19-7-47 dates from 1978 and is directed specifically to aid historical societies with museums.

The Aid to Historical Societies Act (IC 17-3-86) had its

genesis in an act approved March 11, 1901. Subsequent acts in 1921, 1925, and 1927 added the major provisions which were embodied in the 1929 legislation.[7] Since 1929 there have been several amendments mainly concerning how money could be expended and how much money counties could appropriate. The legislation addresses three major issues: capital expenditure, employment of a curator, and annual appropriations for salaries and expenses. The definition of historical society in section 2 is extremely broad. Sections 3 and 4 detail the mechanics of obtaining county aid. It is crucial to note that a society must initiate the procedure by means of a petition; the county commissioners must then recommend to the county council; the council votes upon the recommendation. Sections 5 through 8 deal with the provisions for capital expenditures for physical plant: a maximum of $10,000 with reversion of property safeguards to protect the county's investment. Section 9 specifies the conditions for a county to employ a museum curator for the historical society. This section is relatively meaningless since the counties eligible under the population limits for mandatory employment can vary with each census.[8] Employment of a curator or director in practice falls under the general appropriation provisions in Section 10; the present annual maximum limit is $30,000. Section 10 is the most significant part of this law, and, although accurate information is extremely difficult to obtain, approximately one half of the societies in the state receive some type of aid under it. Only one society, Allen County-Fort Wayne, receives the maximum; average annual aid seems to be around $1,500 to $2,000. It is extremely important to note the variety of uses to which county money can be put and apply those opportunities to the local situation. Most counties which petition for funds with well thought-out programs have been successful; failure to receive money more often reflects a failure to petition than a refusal to appropriate by a county council. The key to success as usual seems to be planning: a good program, groundwork with citizens of the county, and groundwork with the county commissioners, the county council, and the legal advisors to those bodies.

The second statute relating to funding for historical societies, IC 19-7-47, was approved March 7, 1978, and promulgated as Public Law No. 104, Indiana *Acts* 1978. (See below, pp. 96-98). This act is much more specific in its purpose, which is to provide local governmental funding for museums of historical societies. The history of this law is extremely interesting because of the consequences of the amending procedure on the intent of the law. The original law passed in 1978 contained three sections: the first encompassed definitions, the second related to aid by school corporations, and the third related to aid by cities. This law defines historical society very narrowly in terms of purpose and physical plant and specifies the maintenance of a permanent museum; this section has remained as originally enacted. Sections 2 and 3, however, have been very much discussed and, in fact, amended in the 1979 legislature. Public Law No. 199, Indiana *Acts* 1979, was designed to enlarge the scope of IC 19-7-47 to include eligible historical societies throughout the state; the original law contained population limits which made only Allen County school corporations and the cities of Fort Wayne and Gary eligible to use the law. The 1979 amendment did remove population restrictions and enlarged the base for aid by substituting "local governmental unit" for "city" in section 3; it also restricted the school corporation aid to its general fund. This latter move many feel has destroyed the potential effectiveness of section 2 which originally contained the phrase "or any other fund," enabling a school corporation to move to sources not frozen by law as is the general fund. Attempts were made to rectify this omission in the 1980 General Assembly, and they will probably continue until successful. The law is permissive, and opinion generally is that the full weight of the decision to support a local historical society should rest with the local governmental units and not be limited by the General Assembly. The full impact of this law remains to be seen.

With both of these laws the Indiana General Assembly has established permissive statutes that allow a decision on the county or local level regarding support for the work of historical societies. These laws, like all of the other information and funding resources discussed in this article, put the responsibility for initiative and success on individuals and their collective historical consciousness. Indiana government has often been slow in supporting its cultural resources, and the citizens of Indiana have responded in the private sector to serve their needs in such areas. At the present time a wide range and an incredible depth of resources exist in both the public and private sectors. In this time of economic difficulty, and ever increasing demands on the available funds for the support of history and cultural activities, those resources will become less and less adequate. The historical and cultural community must first become aware of the resources at hand; that is the purpose of this article. It remains to assure that these resources adequately serve the needs of those they are designed to help.

LAWS WHICH PROVIDE FUNDING FOR HISTORICAL SOCIETIES
Indiana Code: Title 17, Article 3
Chapter 86. Aid to Historical Societies.

17-3-86-1   Appropriation authorized

Sec. 1. Upon the presentation of a petition as hereinafter provided, the county council of any county contemplated in this act is hereby authorized to make an appropriation of not to exceed ten thousand dollars ($10,000) in the aggregate, out of any money in the general fund of the county treasury not otherwise appropriated, in aid of the historical society of such county, and for the purpose prescribed in section 5 of this act. (*Formerly: Acts 1929, c.42, s.1*).

17-3-86-2   Application of act

Sec. 2.   The provisions of this act shall be construed to apply to any county in this state in which, at the time of the passage of this act, there is a historical society or a local branch of a historical society, or in which such a historical society or a local branch of a historical society may hereafter be established, which, at the time when the petition asking the county council for financial aid is filed, is actively engaged in the collection of data and material for and in the preservation of county and state history and biography, and which holds at least one (1) meeting in each year, at which papers are read or addresses made, in the presence of the public, upon matters connected with the history of the county and state. *(Formerly: Acts 1929, c.42, s.2).*

17-3-86-3   Petitions requesting appropriation

Sec. 3.   The petition requesting the county council to make an appropriation to such historical society or local branch thereof shall be signed by the president and the secretary of such historical society or local branch thereof, and, in addition thereto, by not less than fifty (50) voters and taxpayers who are residents of such county, and shall be presented to the board of commissioners of such county, at any regular session of such board. *(Formerly: Acts 1929, c.42, s.3).*

17-3-86-4   Reference of petition to county council

Sec. 4.   Upon the receipt of such petition, the board of commissioners shall refer such petition to the county council of such county, at a regular or at a called session thereof, with estimates and recommendations as to the amount or amounts of such appropriation or appropriations, in accordance with the provisions of section 19 of an act entitled "An act concerning county business" approved March 3, 1899. *(Formerly: Acts 1929, c.42, s.4).*

17-3-86-5   Limitation on appropriation; purpose of appropriation; construction of rooms, vaults and buildings

Sec. 5.   The appropriation or appropriations made by the county council, in accordance with the provisions of this act, shall not exceed ten thousand dollars ($10,000), in the aggregate, and may be made for the construction and furnishing of rooms or for the purchase and remodeling of a building for the meetings of such historical society; and/or for the installation, construction and furnishing of fireproof vaults for the preservation of the records, historical papers, souvenirs and natural history collections of such society. Such rooms and vaults so constructed, installed, furnished or set aside for and assigned to the society may be in the court-house of such county; or they may be constructed and installed separately upon lands owned by the state or by the county or by any city within such county; or they may be provided, constructed or installed in buildings and on lands which are privately owned and which are leased, rented, donated, given, devised or bequeathed for that purpose; or in buildings and on lands which are purchased and remodeled for that purpose; or in buildings and on lands which are owned by such historical society. Such rooms, vaults and buildings shall be built, constructed, installed, purchased, remodeled or reconstructed and maintained for the purposes enumerated in this act, by the board of commissioners of such county, subject to the provisions and requirements of section 37 of an act entitled "An act concerning county business" approved March 3, 1899. *(Formerly: Acts 1929, c.42, s.5).*

17-3-86-6 Reversion of society property to county

Sec. 6. If the historical society for which and upon whose petition such rooms, vaults or buildings shall have been provided by the county, as prescribed in this act, should fail to avail itself of the use of such rooms, vaults or buildings, or if such historical society shall voluntarily surrender to the county its rights and privileges thereto, or disband, or discontinue its meetings for a period of two (2) consecutive years, all of its papers, records and collections of every kind, and all of its furniture and equipment shall become the property of the county, and the board of county commissioners shall provide for the safekeeping of the same before such rooms, vaults or buildings are used for any other purpose either by the county or by any other person, society or association; but the provisions of this section shall not be so construed as to prevent any person or persons who shall have contributed any papers or historical or biographical data to such collection from making copies thereof for their own private use and profit, nor shall the provisions of this section be so construed as to prevent any person or persons who have lent any object of historical interest or any equipment to the society from recovering possession of such objects of historical interest or equipment. *(Formerly: Acts 1929, c.42, s.6).*

17-3-86-7   Joint control of society buildings; liability for expenses

Sec. 7.   Such rooms, buildings or vaults as may be constructed, purchased, provided or installed in any county of this state, under the provisions of this act, shall be under the joint control of the historical society for the use of which such rooms, vaults, or buildings shall have been provided, and its legitimate successor or successors, and the board of county commissioners, under such rules as they may, by their concurrent action, establish; but such historical society or societies shall alone be responsible for all expenses of every kind incurred in the prosecution of its or their work, except such costs for the construction, purchase, installation and maintenance of the rooms, buildings or vaults and such other expenses as are provided for in this act. *(Formerly: Acts 1929, c.42, s.7).*

17-3-86-8   Forfeiture or voluntary surrender of occupancy; transfer of control to successor society

Sec. 8.   Upon the forfeiture or voluntary surrender of the occupancy of any such rooms, buildings, or vaults to the county, by any historical society for which they were constructed, purchased or installed, the board of county commissioners may place such rooms, buildings or vaults in charge of some other society, organized for purposes similar to those of the original society, if any such society exists in the county, or if any such society shall be organized to the satisfaction of the board; but preference shall, in all cases, be given to the original society, if it should reorganize or resume its activities, and any society that shall accept the use and care of such property and the occupancy of the rooms, buildings or vaults, shall be accountable to the county for the same, and such rooms, buildings and vaults shall continue to be the property of the county as is provided in this act. The purposes of this act are to create and perpetuate a system for the collection and preservation of local and general history, to make a record of the progress of the several counties of the state, and to provide permanent nuclei for individual and family history and local observation of scientific phenomena. *(Formerly: Acts 1929, c.42, s.8)*.

17-3-86-9   Museum curator; appointment; compensation

Sec. 9.   The board of commissioners of any county contemplated in this act may, and in counties of more than twenty-eight thousand (28,000), but less than thirty thousand (30,000) inhabitants according to the last preceding United States census shall employ a museum curator for the historical society of such county. No person shall be appointed curator who has not been recommended by the historical society. The duties of the curator shall be such as may be prescribed by the historical society. The compensation of the curator shall be fixed by the board of county commissioners, upon the recommendation of the historical society. *(Formerly: Acts 1929, c.42, s.9; Acts 1951, c.160, s.1; Acts 1955, c.159, s.1)*.

17-3-86-10   Appropriations for salaries and expenses; limitation

Sec. 10.   For the purpose of paying the curator's salary; printing catalogues of the objects of historical interest, constituting the collection of the society; printing such papers of historical interest as the society may direct; purchasing and installing such equipment as may be deemed to preserve, care for and exhibit the collections of the society; and paying for heat, light, janitor service, rentals, repairs, upkeep, improvements and such other facilities and such help as the society may deem necessary to carry on its work properly, the county council may appropriate whatever sum of money each year that it may deem necessary and expedient not to exceed thirty thousand dollars ($30,000) and which shall be in addition to the appropriation hereinbefore provided for, and which shall be disbursed for the purposes specified in this section, upon the orders of the board of county commissioners, made upon reports of the historical society. *(Formerly: Acts 1929, c.42, s.10; Acts 1955, c.159, s.2; Acts 1959, c.82, s.1; Acts 1963, c.89, s.1).*

17-3-86-11   Construction of act

Sec. 11.   Except as herein otherwise provided, nothing contained in this act shall be so construed as to affect any of the rights, powers, duties or liabilities of any historical or other society contemplated in any or either of the acts which are repealed by this act, or to affect the status, control or jurisdiction of any collection, room, building, vault or other property belonging to and maintained by or for any such society, or to affect the legality of any appropriation which shall have been made under and pursuant to any of the provisions of any or either of the acts which are by this act repealed, but such rights, powers, duties, liabilities, property and appropriations are hereby declared to be preserved unimpaired, except that upon the passage and taking effect of this act, all such historical or other societies and the public officials herein contemplated shall thereafter operate under and be subject to the provisions of this act. *(Formerly: Acts 1929, c.42, s.12).*

Indiana Code: Title 19, Article 7

Chapter 47.   Historical Societies.

19-7-47-1   Definitions

Sec. 1.   Definitions.

"Historical society" means a society which:

(1) is incorporated under the laws of the state of Indiana without stock or purpose of gain to its members;

(2) is organized for the purpose of:

(A) maintaining a permanent historical museum, and

(B) promoting a knowledge of local ancestral heritage and custom; and

(3) owns, possesses, occupies, or maintains a building, grounds, historical artifacts, and equipment.

"Governing body" means any township trustee and the advisory board of a school township, any board of school commissioners, any metropolitan board of education, any board of trustees, or any other board or commission charged by law with the responsibility of administering the affairs of a school corporation.

"School corporation" means any public school corporation established by and under the laws of the state of Indiana. The term includes, but is not necessarily limited to, any school city, school town, school township, consolidated school corporation, metropolitan school district, township school corporation, county school corporation, united school corporation, or any community school corporation. *As added by Acts 1978, P.L.104, SEC.1.*

19-7-47-2   Aid to historical societies by school corporations

Sec. 2.   Aid to Historical Societies by School Corporations. (a) The governing body of a school corporation may pay a historical society a sum of money not to exceed one and one-half cents ($.015) on each one hundred dollars ($100) of assessed value in the school corporation, payable from the general fund of the school corporation.

(b) A historical society may not receive payments from a school corporation unless the board of trustees of the historical society adopts a resolution which gives the governing body of the school corporation the right:

(1) to appoint its superintendent and a history teacher employed by the school corporation as visitors, with the privilege of attending all meetings of the board of trustees of the historical society;

(2) to nominate two (2) persons for membership on the board of trustees of the historical society;

(3) to use any of the historical society's facilities and equipment for educational programs consistent with the purpose of the society;

(4) to send students and teachers of the school corporation on tours of the society's museum, if any, free of charge; and

(5) to borrow historical artifacts from the society's collection, if any, for temporary exhibitions in the schools of the school corporation.

As added by Acts 1978, P.L.104, SEC.1. Amended by Acts 1979, P.L.199, SEC.1

19-7-47-3   Aid to historical societies by local governmental units

Sec. 3.   Aid to Historical Societies by Local Governmental Units. (a) The appropriating authority of a local governmental unit, as that term is defined in IC 18-5-1.5-2, may appropriate to a historical society, a sum of money, not to exceed one and one-half cents ($.015) on each one hundred dollars ($100) of assessed value in the local governmental unit.

(b) A historical society may not receive payments from a local governmental unit described in subsection (a) unless the board of trustees of the historical society adopts a resolution which gives to the chief administrative officer of the local governmental unit the right:

(1) to attend all meetings of the board of trustees of the historical society; and

(2) to nominate two (2) persons for membership on the board of trustees of the historical society.

The resolution must also entitle the inhabitants of the local governmental unit to be admitted to the society's museum, if any, free of charge each Saturday and Sunday during the regular hours. *As added by Acts 1978, P.L.104, SEC.1. Amended by Acts 1979, P.L.199, SEC.2.*

NOTES

1. This article is based upon a handout and presentation compiled for the local history workshops. It is merely an outline of resources; full details on all programs are available from the addresses given.

2. A more detailed statement of the relationship between the Society and the Bureau is given in Pamela J. Bennett, "An Example of State and Private Cooperation: The Indiana Historical Bureau and the Indiana Historical Society," *Indiana History Bulletin,* September, 1978, pp. 123-30.

3. Details of IJHS programs are presented in the February, 1976, and November, 1979, issues of *Indiana History Bulletin.*

4. The Indiana State Archival and Historical Records Plan is printed in the March, 1980, *Indiana History Bulletin.*

5. Sessions on NHPRC were part of the 1979 AASLH program in Tucson, Arizona, and the 1979 SAA program in Chicago, Illinois. See, for example, Larry J. Hackman, "The Historical Records Program: The States and the Nation," in *The American Archivist,* XLIII (1980), 17-32.

6. Through its *Local Library/Local History Newssheet,* an occasional publication sent to all public libraries in the state, the Indiana Historical Society Library has established a forum for the reporting of local history programs at the local level and for suggesting techniques and source materials which will enhance the local history reference function of the local public library.

7. A brief history of the pre-1929 legislation is given in the January, 1929, *Indiana History Bulletin,* pp. 65-66.

8. The population limits were added in a 1951 amendment. Counties eligible according to the 1950 Census of Population were Clinton, Hamilton, Jackson, Marshall, Miami, Montgomery, Shelby, and Wabash. Only Dearborn and Randolph counties qualify according to the 1970 Census of Population figures. Information on the effectiveness of this section since 1951 has not been compiled.

APPENDIX

The following is a list of organizations and libraries represented at three 1979 local history workshops.

Region 3 (Lafayette)

    Anson Wolcott Historical Society
    Benton County Historical Society
    Cass County Historical Society
    Clinton County Historical Society
    Howard County Museum
    Montgomery County Historical Society
    Tippecanoe County Historical Society
    Warren County Historical Society
    White County Historical Society

Region 4 (Anderson)

    Carmel-Clay Historical Society
    Hamilton County Historical Society
    Hancock County Historical Society
    Henry County Historical Society
    Jay County Historical Society
    Madison County Historical Society
    Tipton County Historical Society

Region 7 (Oldenburg)

    Dearborn County Historical Society
    Franklin County Historical Society
    Hillforest Historical Foundation, Inc.
    Historic Connersville, Inc.
    Ripley County Historical Society
    Sisters of St. Francis Convent

Region 1 (Valparaiso)

    The East Chicago Historical Society was inadvertently left off the list on page 85 of the first volume of *Local History Today* of organizations that attended the Region 1 Workshop.